T0328591

Cambridge Elements ≡

Elements in Bioethics and Neuroethics
edited by
Thomasine Kushner
California Pacific Medical Center, San Francisco

WHAT PLACEBOS TEACH US ABOUT HEALTH AND CARE

A Philosopher Pops a Pill

Dien Ho
*Massachusetts College of Pharmacy
and Health Sciences*

CAMBRIDGE
UNIVERSITY PRESS

Shaftesbury Road, Cambridge CB2 8EA, United Kingdom

One Liberty Plaza, 20th Floor, New York, NY 10006, USA

477 Williamstown Road, Port Melbourne, VIC 3207, Australia

314–321, 3rd Floor, Plot 3, Splendor Forum, Jasola District Centre, New Delhi – 110025, India

103 Penang Road, #05–06/07, Visioncrest Commercial, Singapore 238467

Cambridge University Press is part of Cambridge University Press & Assessment, a department of the University of Cambridge.

We share the University's mission to contribute to society through the pursuit of education, learning and research at the highest international levels of excellence.

www.cambridge.org
Information on this title: www.cambridge.org/9781009454452

DOI: 10.1017/9781009085496

First published 2023

A catalogue record for this publication is available from the British Library

ISBN 978-1-009-45445-2 Hardback
ISBN 978-1-009-08793-3 Paperback
ISSN 2752-3934 (online)
ISSN 2752-3926 (print)

What Placebos Teach Us about Health and Care

A Philosopher Pops a Pill

Elements in Bioethics and Neuroethics

DOI: 10.1017/9781009085496
First published online: September 2023

Dien Ho
Massachusetts College of Pharmacy and Health Sciences
Author for correspondence: Dien Ho, dien.ho@mcphs.edu

Abstract: Placebo effects raise some fundamental questions concerning the nature of clinical and medical research. This Element begins with an overview of the different roles placebos play, followed by a survey of significant studies and dominant views about placebo mechanisms. It then critically examines the concept of *placebo* and offers a new definition that avoids the pitfalls of other attempts. The main philosophical lesson is that background medical theories provide the ontology for clinical and medical research. Because these theories often contain incoherent and arbitrary classifications, the concept of *placebo* inherits the same messiness. The Element concludes by highlighting some impending challenges for placebo studies.

Keywords: placebo, philosophy of medicine, placebo therapy, health humanities, healthcare

ISBNs: 9781009454452 (HB), 9781009087933 (PB), 9781009085496 (OC)
ISSNs: 2752-3934 (online), 2752-3926 (print)

Contents

Introduction

The most used effective medical treatment in the history of humanity is the placebo. My confidence stems from the fact that, prior to the advent of modern medicine, most treatments were of marginal benefit. When they did improve patients' conditions, it was overwhelmingly likely due to their placebo effects. Yet, the paltry amount that has been written on placebos in medicine and in philosophy hardly reflects their centrality in how we heal. Placebos have always sat outside conventional medicine. They serve as controls in clinical experiments – a tool to help determine if a treatment is effective – but are rarely the subject of trials themselves. In clinical medicine, placebos have been used to placate anxious patients or to induce psychological benefits through deception. It is unsurprising that placebos carry a certain stigma that makes taking them seriously a difficult task. The main purpose of this Element is to question some of the common beliefs about placebos. The lessons learned not only destigmatize placebos; they also tell us a great deal about the institution of medicine, health, and the art of healing.

The first three sections of the Element provide an empirically informed background for the philosophical discussion of placebo in the fourth section, where we will closely examine how to define *placebo*. In Section 1, I introduce the history, terminology, and conceptual distinctions concerning placebos and placebo effects. Although placebos often involve pharmaceuticals, there are other placebo interventions including sham surgeries and placebo psychotherapies. Given my research orientation, I often default to pharmaceuticals to mine examples. In Section 2, I present a curated survey of some of the most fascinating clinical results on placebos. The main aim is to bring placebo effects into better focus so that we can delineate the boundaries of what researchers consider as placebo effects. In Section 3, I explore some of the leading views of placebo mechanisms. While researchers have long considered classical conditioning and expectancy to be the most plausible candidates, the recent emergence of the Bayesian brain model provides a more comprehensive and viable alternative. Although I include philosophical discussions in the first three sections, Section 4 engages with some of the deepest conceptual issues. One of these is an explanation of why providing a satisfactory definition of *placebo* has proven to be so utterly elusive. The reason, I argue, lies in how background medical theories determine the micro-ontology of medicine (e.g., what constitutes the defining characteristic of a treatment). Given the often incoherent and arbitrary distinctions embedded in these theories, a definition of *placebo* inherits the same messiness. I also offer my attempt to define *placebo* in this section. The final section outlines some of the immediate empirical and conceptual issues that, I believe, ought to be addressed in placebo study.

1 History and Conceptual Landscape

1.1 Overdosing on Placebos

A twenty-six-year-old man, Mr. A, arrived at the emergency department of the Veterans Affairs Hospital in Jackson, Mississippi.[1] Before collapsing, he muttered, "Help me, I took all my pills." His hand held an empty pill bottle from an antidepressant clinical trial in which he was enrolled. He had taken its entire content in a suicide attempt. Mr. A's blood pressure was 80/40 (about half that of a healthy adult) and he had an elevated heart rate of 110 beats per minute. He was also pale and sweating profusely. A physician from the trial arrived soon afterward and confirmed that Mr. A was in the control arm of the study; he had ingested twenty-nine placebo pills. On learning the news, Mr. A was relieved and, within fifteen minutes, his blood pressure returned to 126/80 with a heart rate of 80. The official diagnosis: hypotension due to a placebo overdose.

The causal power of the placebo pills was surely one remarkable fact about the case. Dropping one's blood pressure by almost 50 percent with the help of these pills is impressive, especially when standard drugs such as ACE (angiotensin-converting enzyme) inhibitors lower blood pressure only by about 5 percent. A closer examination of Mr. A's story reveals a host of further puzzles about placebos and their effects. For instance, a placebo is commonly referred to as an inert intervention. If placebo pills were indeed inert, Mr. A's case would be logically impossible; inert pills, read literally, cannot cause anything.

Did Mr. A overdose on placebos? Suppose the control pills that Mr. A took were made of starch. Surely, Mr. A did not ingest a harmful quantity of starch. Whatever caused Mr. A's symptoms, the very substance that made up the control pills seemed to matter little. If Mr. A had overdosed on placebos, it was likely not due to the fact that he took too much starch; instead, it was because he went through the motion of ingesting pills too many times. It was this overdoing that caused his dramatic hypotension. If this is right, then the cause was not the pills per se; it was the beliefs (or even just the rituals and performatives) concerning the pills that prompted Mr. A's symptoms. The pills played but a small part in this grand performance.

If the cause of the placebogenic overdose was the belief that he had swallowed a fatal dose, then the specific act of taking the pills was equally not necessary. Anything that led to the formation of the belief would be sufficient to bring about the placebo effects. Suppose through intense rumination (a kind of deliberate self-delusion) one can form the thoughts that generate placebo effects. If so, the presence of *any* physical placebo intervention (pills, performatives, and so on) would be unnecessary. This picture presupposes that beliefs are sufficient for placebo effects. However, a number of studies have raised the possibility that even beliefs might not be necessary. A study by Karin Jensen et al. concludes that placebo effects can be elicited by visual stimuli that fall below the threshold of conscious recognition.[2] Similarly, subjects in trials exploring the therapeutic use of open-label placebos (OLP, i.e., placebo therapies in which patients are fully aware that they are being treated with placebos) often do not hold any beliefs that the placebos will be effective. The very ritual of ingesting pills might provide therapeutic benefits. Of course, to figure out what we should think about placebos in light of these clinical trials requires that we first decide whether the effects are placebogenic. And to do that we need to have a clear understanding of what constitutes a placebo effect.

The idea that thoughts can generate physiological changes is not surprising. My belief that I ought to lose some weight might lead me to adopt a better diet which, in turn, leads me to have lower blood pressure. No one would find the possibility of this belief-initiated causal chain that ends with measurable results remotely mysterious. Of course, the diet example requires the causal chain to "go outside" the body; I have to eat different food in order to bring about physiological changes. The very thought of having committed a fatal overdose was enough to cause Mr. A's blood pressure to drop by 50 percent. The entire causal process took place inside Mr. A. But, this too is not a good way to distinguish placebogenic effects from nonplacebogenic ones. By focusing on a particularly stressful experience, I may be able to increase my heart rate, cause profuse sweating, and even raise my blood pressure. What then distinguishes a causal pathway of a placebo effect from a nonplacebo one?

These quick reflections suggest that the concepts of *placebo* and *placebo effect* are hardly well defined. The main claim of this Element is that the challenges encountered in defining placebo and placebo effect stem from conceptual inconsistencies and the arbitrariness of background medical theories and ontology (i.e., how we categorize diseases, treatments, and so on). In this sense, the philosophical questions raised in placebo research tell as much about the nature of placebos as they do about medicine in general. In establishing this conclusion, my strategy is to first introduce some results from empirical studies (Section 2) and the dominant views of the placebo mechanism (Section 3) so that we have a sense of what researchers and clinicians consider as placebo effects. In Section 4, after examining some unsuccessful attempts to define placebo and placebo effects, I will offer an alternate definition. I hope readers can forgive the delayed formulation of an explicit definition.

Philosophy can help clear the conceptual underbrush so that research and clinical medicine can better avoid conceptual confusions, wasted resources, and flawed methodologies. My hope is that a critical examination of the nature of placebo will lead to better medicine. If beneficial placebo effects stem from, say, our body's autonomic responses to external cues (e.g., being cared for), expanding the boundaries of treatments to incorporate the therapeutic power of these cues can produce more therapeutic tools and help improve health outcomes.

1.2 The Three-Fold Distinction of Placebo

Within clinical discourse, the term "placebo" refers to three different usages: as a means to placate anxious patients, as controls for clinical trials, and as therapies. This three-fold distinction will structure our introduction to placebo.

Historically, placebos were given by clinicians to placate patients, to make them less anxious about their ailments. The ailments were usually not related to anxiety per se. It could be that a patient experiences some gastrointestinal problems and the inability to control them causes anxiety. By giving the patient a placebo intervention, the clinician does not believe that the intervention can address the gastrointestinal problems; instead, they believe that it can soothe the patient's nerves. Perhaps the very act of doing *something* lessens the patient's anxiety.

By the middle of the twentieth century, placebos gained a new prominence. As researchers became more aware of the dramatic effects of the mere act of administering an intervention, the need to conduct controlled clinical trials to ascertain the true effectiveness of a treatment grew. One classic method of accomplishing this is to use John Stuart Mill's Method of Difference by comparing the investigative objects against controls that "have every circumstance in common save one."[3] In a clinical trial, an ideal placebo control includes all aspects of the experimental treatment except the treatment itself.

Finally, recent research suggests that placebos can confer therapeutic benefits. Unlike the first usage of placebos to placate patients, therapeutic placebos aim to address specific ailments, as opposed to the anxiety of being ill. It is worth noting that placebo therapies represent a departure from conventional medicine. Typically, medical treatments are introduced from the outside to cause some physiological changes in the patient. From the introduction of a pharmaceutical to surgical manipulation, modern medicine requires some external elements to make you feel better. Placebo therapies, on the other hand, rely entirely on resources that the body already possesses.

These three usages of placebos might be about the same thing or they might refer to three distinct types of thing that happen to share the same label. There are some prima facie reasons to lean toward the latter view. As I suggest in Section 5, researchers' incentive to minimize the effectiveness of the placebo arm might lead to experimental biases. The therapeutic use of placebos, however, is exactly the opposite. An effective placebo treatment would presumably be as causally efficacious as possible. The fact that these two uses of placebos have radically opposing aims should make us wonder if they ultimately concern the same thing.

To enable greater clarity in our discussion of these competing senses and applications of the term, I will introduce placebo and placebo effect in terms of the three usages – placebos-to-placate, placebos-as-controls, and placebos-as-therapies – in the remainder of this section. The history of placebo fortunately mirrors the tripartite distinction such that an examination of the concept of *placebo* can proceed chronologically. This introduction will give a basic sense of how the term "placebo" is used in medicine and help mark out, roughly, the subject of our investigation.

1.3 Placebos to Placate

The Latin term "placebo" simply means "I shall please." During a typical Medieval funeral service, participants would often recite Psalm 114 of the Latin Vulgate Bible which ends with the line: "Placebo Domino in regione vivorum," meaning "I will please the Lord in the land of the living."[4] Because food was often served at these services, funeral crashers would sing along in the hope of free refreshments. These pretend mourners became known as "placebo singers." Their dubious reputation makes an appearance in Chaucer's *The Merchant Tale* in the form of the sycophant Placebo who flatters the protagonist Januarie by incessantly affirming his beliefs.

The practice of giving patients placebos in order to placate them was hardly a rare practice. In Robert Hooper's 1817 medical dictionary *Quincy's Lexicon Medicum*, "placebo" is defined as "an epithet given to any medicine adapted more to please than benefit the patient."[5] Clinicians such as W. R. Houston suggest that past medical treatments could very well have conferred benefits to patients but not through their alleged causal pathways.[6] Bygone treatments survived because they did make patients feel better via their placebogenic ability to alleviate anxiety. These positive placebogenic effects or what Thomas Jefferson called "pious fraud" masked the ineffectiveness of the intended therapies and ensured their continual prescription.

The practice of prescribing placebos to ease patients' anxiety continues to the present day. Of 231 physicians surveyed, Sherman and Hickner report that 45 percent had used placebos in their clinical practice and 18 percent prescribed placebos in order to "calm the patient."[7] Often, clinicians prescribe placebos that are neither causally inert (e.g., antibiotics) nor therapeutically indicated.

This description of placebos-as-pacifiers hides a deep tension. If an alleged treatment is ineffective, how could it make patients feel better? Alternatively, if patients feel better, were the treatments not effective? As we will see, this tension hints at the need to reexamine our understanding of disease, treatment, and the very aim of healing. We will return to these issues in Section 4.

1.4 Placebos as Controls

Although medical researchers have long employed placebo-controlled experiments, until the middle of the twentieth century evidence for the effectiveness of most medical treatments was largely not based on comparative clinical trials. Anecdotal evidence played a far greater role. The use of placebo as trial control gained significant acceptance by the middle of the twentieth century and much of the credit goes to Henry Beecher and his article "The Powerful Placebo."[8] In this meta-analysis of fifteen clinical studies, Beecher concluded that approximately 35 percent of the time, placebos provided satisfactory responses. These included the use of saline for analgesic purposes and baking soda for chest pain. Given the effectiveness of placebos, Beecher writes:

> It should be apparent that "clinical impression" is hardly a dependable source of information without the essential safeguards of the double unknowns technique, the use of placebos also as unknowns, randomization of administration, the use of correlated data … and mathematical validation of any supposed differences …. To separate out even fairly great true effects above those of a placebo is manifestly difficult to impossible on the basis of clinical impression. Many a drug has been extolled on the basis of clinical impression when the only power it had was that of a placebo.[9]

To measure the exact therapeutic effectiveness of a treatment, it is paramount that double-blind randomized clinical trials compare the experimental treatment against a counterpart that resembles it in as many respects as possible other than the presence of the treatment itself; that is, we control the comparison with a suitable placebo.

To be sure, one can investigate the effectiveness of a therapy by pitting it against an existing treatment. Active-controlled trials (i.e., trials that use a treatment as a control) are an indispensable method in clinical experimentation and this is particularly so for ethical reasons. As the use of placebo control gained prominence, the World Medical Association's 1964 *Declaration of Helsinki* specified researchers' ethical obligation to provide subjects in all arms of a clinical trial with interventions that are no worse than existing treatments. Placebo controls are permissible, according to the Helsinki standards, only if there are no existing treatments or if their usages are scientifically necessary and subjects are not irreversibly and seriously harmed. The *Declaration of Helsinki* in essence states that the epistemic benefits of a placebo-controlled trial do not

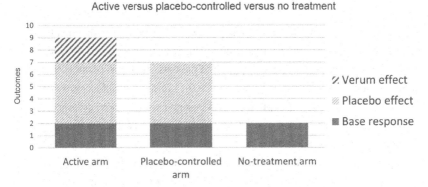

Figure 1 An example of the additive model

outweigh the potential harm inflicted on subjects who receive no treatments. Notice that the *Declaration* assumes that subjects in a placebo-controlled arm do not receive any treatments. If the placebo controls provide therapeutic benefits, the obligation not to expose subjects to no treatment becomes less obvious. One might imagine that a placebo control might outperform the standard treatment. In this case, not only would the use of a placebo control be ethically permissible, it might even be obligatory.

The idea that the effectiveness of an experimental treatment is the difference between the outcome of an active arm and the outcome of the placebo-controlled arm is known as the additive model. Figure 1 shows that the net effectiveness (or verum effectiveness) of the experimental treatment is two units. It is imperative that one does not confuse the outcome of the placebo-controlled arm with placebo effects. The outcome of the control arm contains two parts: placebo effects and base response. In addition to placebo effects, some of the positive outcome comes from factors that have nothing to do with placebo effects – referred to here as "base response." They include the natural history of the disease, regression to the mean, ebbing of negative effects from previous treatments, spontaneous remission (i.e., the diminishing of some pathology that is unrelated to any salient treatment), and symptoms fluctuations. Subjects in a two-week trial investigating the effectiveness of a treatment for the common cold, for instance, would likely improve during the course of the trial since most common colds last five days or so. Those who are in the placebo-controlled arm will report improved outcomes that may have nothing to do with placebo effects. Conflating the outcome of the placebo-controlled arm with placebo effects is surprisingly common in clinical scholarship; Beecher makes that very mistake in his 1955 paper.[10] To determine the exact magnitude of placebo effects in the control arm, it must be compared to one consisting of no treatment.

1.5 Placebos as Therapies

The idea of intentionally prescribing placebos to patients for therapeutic purposes, as opposed to merely placating them, has long been recognized to be ethically problematic. Placebos work only if patients are deceived about their true nature, so the conventional view goes. Given the premium we place on safeguarding patients' autonomy, deceptive placebo usage certainly runs contrary to this commitment. In the domain of medical research, some scholars have suggested the use of "authorized deception" to alleviate some of the ethical concerns.[11] The idea is that participants are told at the outset of the study that they might not be given the whole truth – some information might be withheld by the investigators. By consenting to the study, subjects have thus consented to being deceived and their autonomy is preserved (i.e., they *chose* to be deceived). By agreeing to be "fooled," one's autonomy is not compromised, much like attending a magic show.

An obvious problem with "authorized deception" is that a vague warning of deception might not be informative enough to provide meaningful consent. Of course, if a patient is convinced that their care provider knows them well enough, they might trust that their care provider would not do anything that they would object to (had they known the whole truth). Nonetheless, when clinical encounters are brief and sustained relationships between patients and doctors are rare, it is difficult to cultivate the familiarity necessary to justify therapeutic paternalism in the form of authorized deception.

A different attempt to meet the ethical challenges of placebo therapies is to jettison the entire practice of deception altogether. Recent research has shown that placebo effects might emerge even if subjects knew they were receiving placebos (i.e., OLPs). In one of the earliest OLP therapy trials, Adrian Sandler, Corrine Glesne, and James Bodfish observed eighty children aged between six and twelve who were receiving stimulants for their attention deficit hyperactivity disorder (ADHD).[12] The children were randomly assigned to three arms for an eight-week study. In the control arm, participants received full doses of stimulants. In the second arm, participants received full doses for four weeks followed by a dose reduced by 50 percent for four weeks. In the third arm, participants received full doses for four weeks along with a visually distinctive OLP and, for the remaining four weeks, they took a 50 percent reduced dose of the stimulant along with the same placebo pill. Parents, teachers (who were unaware of the children's treatment status), and the study's clinicians measured the outcome and they observed no significant difference in the severity of ADHD symptoms between children receiving their normal dose of stimulants and those receiving a 50 percent dosage plus the placebo. In contrast, the symptoms were significantly more severe in children who received 50 percent reduced doses of the stimulant without the accompanying placebo. The study hints at the possibility that ADHD medications can maintain their effectiveness at 50 percent dosage when they are paired with a placebo. This is the case even if subjects are aware that the placebo "dose extender" contains no drug.

Researcher Ted Kaptchuk has conducted some of the most important and extensive studies on the therapeutic benefits of OLPs. In their pilot study, Kaptchuk et al. examined the effectiveness of OLPs to treat irritable bowel syndrome (IBS).[13] The choice of IBS was very much a deliberate one. Not only is IBS one of the most common functional bowel disorders, but there are few, if any, treatments. Furthermore, the pathophysiology and etiology of IBS are poorly understood. Like many gastrointestinal ailments, psychosocial factors appear to play a role, along with immune activation, inflammation, and genetic dispositions. Many of these factors lie along the gut–brain axis making IBS ideal for an investigation into harnessing placebos' power to alter physiology via psychological and behavioral triggers. The key question is whether placebos can help even if patients are fully aware of their nature.

Between 2009–10, Kaptchuk's team conducted a three-week randomized controlled trial in which eighty patients were randomly placed into two groups: an OLP group and a no-treatment or treatment-as-usual group. Patients who had been taking IBS medication for more than thirty days prior to the start of the study were allowed to continue their usual treatments. The group that received OLPs were told that the placebo was "an inactive (i.e., "inert") substance like a sugar pill that contained no medication." The team then read a script emphasizing four key points: "1) the placebo effect is powerful, 2) the body can automatically respond to taking placebo pills like Pavlov's dogs who salivated when they heard a bell, 3) a positive attitude helps but is not necessary, and 4) taking the pills faithfully is critical."[14]

At the midpoint and the endpoint of the trial, patients reported their IBS conditions by completing surveys that measured global improvement of their condition, severity of their symptoms, whether they received adequate relief, and their general quality of life. The results were promising. Overall, patients who were in the open-label arm did significantly better than those in the no-treatment or treatment-as-usual arm across all four metrics.

Kaptchuk et al.'s OLP trial for IBS upends the assumption that deception is necessary for placebo response. To be sure, clinical trials with larger cohorts across multiple trial centers are needed before placebos become a part of our treatment toolbox. But the fact that investigators can elicit therapeutic placebo responses without deception circumvents one of the central ethical constraints limiting the use of placebos in clinical settings.

The inclusion of therapeutic placebos into our pharmacological formularies such that clinicians can prescribe them, insurance providers cover their cost, and retail pharmacies properly dispense them will require a great deal of rethinking about placebos, drugs, and treatments in general. Currently, health insurers typically do not cover placebos, even for use in clinical trials. The popular reference guide *Facts and Comparisons* that pharmacists rely on does not contain an entry on placebos. And, if hopeful expectation is a contributing component of effective placebos, every key person along the therapeutic journey would ideally be trained to convey its importance.

Placebo therapies force us to reconsider the metaphysics of treatments. Typically, a drug's therapeutic effect is divided into two categories: specific versus nonspecific actions. Aspirin's ability to block the production of the lipid prostaglandins that are critical in promoting pain and inflammation is its specific action. On the other hand, the mere act of taking an aspirin might also mitigate pain by encouraging the production of endogenous opioids. This placebogenic analgesic effect would thus be a nonspecific action. It takes the briefest of reflection to recognize that the distinction between specific and nonspecific actions is hardly clear. Some of the difficulties, as I will argue in Section 4, have far deeper implications. For example, if contextual factors, from clinicians' enthusiasm to the color of a pill, affect the effectiveness of a drug, should we count them among the active ingredients? If medicine helps us live a fulfilling and satisfying life, does it matter whether or not the means come from the active ingredients?

1.6 Three Kinds of Placebos?

To end this section, I briefly summarize that the history of placebos marks three distinct usages. First, placebos have consisted of interventions that are given to placate anxious patients. Second, placebos have been used as a control equivalent in clinical trials; that is, a placebo is "everything but the study's target." Finally, recent studies have shown that placebos might confer therapeutic benefits for specific conditions. As opposed to merely placating patients, this notion of placebo more closely resembles our traditional concept of a *treatment*.

Although scholars have noted the variety of placebo uses, the distinctions have not been identified explicitly. Furthermore, philosophical and clinical scholarship has largely treated these three senses of "placebo" as concerning one type of thing. It might be the case that there is a single notion of placebo and that it can be used in these different ways. But, as mentioned earlier, there are reasons to be cautious. What these three usages have in common, however, is that placebo effects involve cognitive changes that cause physiological changes.

In the most obvious case, the belief that one is receiving an analgesic lessens the intensity of pain. But even this straightforward example raises some immediate puzzles. If a placebo lessens someone's pain, why is it not an analgesia on a par with other pain medications? Should analgesia be defined in terms of a class of causal pathways so that placebo analgesics are excluded? What makes these pathways different? Given the contemporary research focus on placebos as controls for clinical trials and as therapeutic options, the remainder of the Element will primarily investigate these two uses.

The next two sections will continue to build an empirical foundation for an informed philosophical discussion on placebos. Section 2 introduces some significant clinical trials that tell us a great deal about placebo effects. In addition, they will also help mark out what researchers consider as placebo effects, which will anchor our conceptual analysis by identifying some pretheoretical usages of "placebo" and "placebo effect." Section 3 examines three prominent views of the mechanisms responsible for placebo effects. Understanding the strengths and weaknesses of these will help identify the physiology of placebo effects and help determine if there is a fundamental difference between placebogenic effects and nonplacebogenic ones. If it turns out to be the case that placebo therapies rely on "contextual factors" such as the demeanor of the clinician or the price point of the treatment, how does that affect what we think treatments in general consist of? This will connect the philosophy of clinical and medical research to the day-to-day practice of healthcare.

2 A Survey of Placebo Studies

2.1 Why These Studies Matter

Although placebos have been an indispensable part of controlled clinical trials, investigations into the physiological mechanisms and the therapeutic use of placebos have emerged only in the last twenty years or so. And, as with any new field, there are fundamental conceptual issues that need to be clarified. A question as straightforward as "What sort of physiological response constitutes a *placebo* response?" is certainly not settled. The curated presentation of clinical studies in this section aims to give an overview of what we currently know about placebo effects. Not only do these studies shed light on how placebos work, they also present some fascinating and unexpected results. First, these studies illustrate the causal pathways of placebo effects. Placebogenic analgesia, for instance, turns out to be far more complex than researchers had expected. Second, the assumption that deception is necessary to elicit placebo effects has been found to be false. Third, placebo effects can generate objective measurable results that go beyond subjects' reports of pain, anxiety, and so on. As with any broad survey, the choice of what to include is clearly subjective. Moreover, given the relatively recent emergence of placebo studies and the limited sample size of many trials, it behooves us not to leap to generalizations.

2.2 The Start of the Modern Placebo Discussion

No other publication has perhaps generated as much interest in placebos and inspired as much change in the design of clinical trials as Henry Beecher's 1955 iconic piece "The Powerful Placebo." The story goes that Beecher was serving as a battlefield medic in World War II when seasoned nurses and doctors told him that if he ran out of morphine, an injection of saline would work about a third of the time. Beecher was thus introduced to the analgesic power of placebos. Upon returning to the United States, he proclaimed the importance of comparing standard treatments against placebo-controlled arms to ascertain the treatments' true effectiveness. Any treatment might produce positive outcomes because of its placebo effect; the only way to tell if a treatment does what it claims is to compare it to a placebo equivalent.

Although this story of how Beecher became fascinated with placebos has been told many times over, there is no evidence that it actually happened. Indeed, in his earlier article "Pain in Men Wounded in Battle," published in the *Annals of Surgery*, the analgesic power of saline or of any other placebos is completely absent.[15] It is all the more puzzling since the piece's central claim is that morphine is overused in battlefields: wounded soldiers often look dreadful but they are not in pain and their agitation can be better treated via other means.

The overall structure of Beecher's 1955 article is straightforward. It consists of a review of fifteen studies on conditions ranging from seasickness to postoperative pain. Each of these studies compares the effectiveness of a treatment against a placebo control. Beecher then pools together the studies and calculates the overall magnitude of the placebo effect. The percentage of subjects who experience satisfactory improvement in the placebo-controlled arm in these studies range from 15 percent to 58 percent. Beecher thus concludes that placebos "have a high degree of therapeutic effectiveness in treating subjective responses ... in $35.2 \pm 2.2\%$ of cases."[16] The lesson to be learned, Beecher suggests, is that clinical trials that aim to determine the therapeutic effect of a treatment ought to satisfy the following:

(1) Subjects are randomly assigned to experimental arms;
(2) Neither the clinicians nor the subjects know which arm they belong to (i.e., double-blinded); and,
(3) Inclusion of a placebo-controlled arm.

Without these safeguards, Beecher argues, subjective biases and placebo effects could give a false picture of a treatment's effectiveness.

The existence and magnitude of placebo effects remained largely unchallenged until a meta-analysis by Asbjørn Hróbjartsson and Peter Gøtzsche[17]— a study that we will look at shortly. Beecher's article, however, contains some fairly obvious shortcomings. To begin with, he does not offer any rationale for the choice of the fifteen studies. Before the publication of "The Powerful Placebo" in 1955, there had already been hundreds of clinical trials that used placebo controls. Without an argument to justify the selection of these specific fifteen studies, Beecher risks cherry-picking his data. Furthermore, it is unclear whether the assignment of subjects to experimental arms was randomized or whether clinicians and subjects were able to remain blinded throughout the duration of the studies. Considering Beecher's conclusion that good clinical trials are randomized and double-blinded, the use of studies that did not satisfy these criteria (including one conducted by Beecher) is at best methodologically awkward.

In 1997, Gunver Kienle and Helmut Kiene took a closer look at Beecher's fifteen trials to determine if his conclusion was warranted. In addition to identifying a number of basic mistakes (e.g., Beecher misquoted key results in ten of the fifteen studies, including one in which he served as a coinvestigator), the authors argue that in "none of these trials was there any reason to assume the existence of the slightest placebo effect ... on the basis of the published data, in all of these trials the reported outcome in the placebo groups can be fully, plausibly, and easily explained *without* presuming any therapeutic placebo effect."[18] In Section 1, I suggested that some researchers falsely assume that improvements in the placebo-controlled arm constitute placebo effects: that is, positive outcomes in the placebo-controlled arm can be due to nonplacebo factors including the natural history of the disease, fluctuation of symptoms, and the ebbing of the toxic effects of previous treatments. Beecher does indeed commit the very sin of conflating placebo effects with positive outcomes in the control arm. Kienle and Kiene argue that Beecher did not rule out the possibility that the positive outcomes in these trials were due to the plethora of non-placebogenic causes. Still, the conclusion they draw is rather premature. The fact that alternate and nonplacebogenic explanations existed does not mean that there were *no* placebo effects. It merely means that Beecher was not warranted in concluding that placebo effects existed in these trials.

One further curious note: Kienle and Kiene claim, as many researchers do, that spontaneous improvements among subjects in the control arm is an instance of positive outcomes that are not placebo effects. This assumption, however, requires a closer examination. Consider spontaneous regression (SR) in cancer care defined as the disappearance of a tumor without treatment.[19] Suppose, in a clinical trial, some of the subjects in the control arm who received placebos develop SR. Is the SR a placebo effect? The answer depends on the causal path of the regression. For instance, if the regression was ultimately caused by the fact that the subjects drank orange juice for breakfast and that, unbeknownst to the researchers, the chemical composition of orange juice led to changes in the subjects' immune system which caused it to attack the tumor cells, then it certainly seems that the SR was not placebogenic. On the other hand, suppose that the mere act of injecting the experimental drug caused the subjects' immune systems to attack the tumor cells, then it is far more natural to say that the eventual SR was a placebo effect. This quick thought experiment hints at the idea that the underlying physiological causal path plays an important role in how we identify a placebo effect.

2.3 Multiple Pathways of Placebo Analgesia

Researchers have long suspected that individuals' expectations of certain outcomes and classical conditioning cause placebo effects. In a 2017 study, Ricardo de la Vega et al. measured how long it took sixty college students to run 200 meters.[20] A week later, the students returned and were given a green color energy drink. One group was told that the drink would improve their performance, another group that it might or might not improve performance, and a third group was told there was no evidence the drink would provide any boost. After consuming the drink, subjects again ran 200 meters. Those in the first group not only thought they had run faster; their average time was a statistically significant 6 percent better. The other two groups did not experience any meaningful improvements. Numerous other experiments have shown a robust relationship between expectation and placebo responses.

Researchers also suspect that classical conditioning might account for some placebo responses. Classical conditioning involves the creation of an association between a stimulus that naturally leads to some involuntary response with a neutral stimulus. Pavlov's dog, for instance, associated the presence of food, which caused it to salivate, with the ringing of a bell. After repeated exposure, the dog began to salivate when the bell was rung even without the presence of food. Placebo effects, some researchers have argued, follow a similar model. In numerous clinical investigations, subjects go through a conditioning phase in which neutral stimuli (e.g., the application of a cream) accompany unconditioned stimuli (e.g., the application of heat) to generate placebo effects. The unconditioned stimuli cause some involuntary response (e.g., pain) and after sufficient pairing between the neutral stimuli and the unconditioned stimuli, subjects experience the involuntary response with the mere presence of the neutral stimuli (e.g., they experience warmth when the cream is applied without the application of heat). One might consider the involuntary response a placebo or nocebo (an undesired response) effect.

In an ambitious twelve-arm experiment, Martina Amanzio and Fabrizio Benedetti aimed to test the expectation and conditioning hypotheses and to uncover the underlying physiology of placebogenic analgesia.[21] With the use of a tourniquet and a sphygmomanometer, blood flow was cut off in the nondominant arms of the subjects who were then asked to squeeze a hand-exerciser. The burning pain followed immediately, and subjects were asked to squeeze until the pain became unbearable (usually under fourteen minutes). Meanwhile, an intravenous (IV) line was attached to the dominant arm where a hidden pump introduced saline, morphine (an opioid analgesic), or ketorolac (a nonsteroid anti-inflammatory drug that has no effects on opioid receptors). The purpose was to induce placebogenic analgesia through either expectation or conditioning. Finally, naloxone (an opioid receptor blocker) was introduced to some subjects to determine whether all placebogenic analgesia travels along an opioid pathway.

The results of the study were stunning. As shown in a previous study conducted by Jon Levine, Newton Gordon, and Howard Fields,[22] Amanzio and Benedetti confirmed that placebogenic analgesia (induced by expectation) can be canceled out by the introduction of naloxone. This strongly suggests that some placebogenic analgesia functions along the endogenous opioid path. For subjects who were conditioned with morphine, Amanzio and Benedetti noted robust pain tolerance when they were injected with saline and were told that the injection was not an analgesic. More importantly, the pain tolerance was higher for subjects who were both conditioned and told that they were receiving a morphine injection than for those who were merely conditioned. This suggests that conditioning and expectation can work on top of one another. Furthermore, when naloxone was introduced surreptitiously, it completely eliminated any placebogenic analgesic effect regardless of whether it was induced by conditioning or conditioning and expectation. This suggests that placebo analgesia caused by morphine conditioning and expectation functions along the exact same opioid pathway.

For subjects who were conditioned with ketorolac (a nonsteroidal anti-inflammatory drug or NSAID with no opioid action) instead of morphine, the results were even more astonishing. Like the morphine groups, conditioning (with ketorolac) and expectation seem to have an additive property. Unlike the group conditioned with morphine, when naloxone was introduced it only partially diminished the placebogenic analgesia. And, when subjects who were conditioned with ketorolac had no expectation that a later saline injection could relieve pain, naloxone had no impact on the subjects' pain tolerance. In other words, naloxone could not cancel the conditioning-induced analgesia using ketorolac. This suggests that the conditioned placebogenic analgesia, established using an NSAID, travels along a nonopioid pathway. The obvious conclusion is that not all placebogenic analgesic mechanisms are the same. Expectation-generated placebogenic analgesia appears to depend on some endogenous opioid mechanism. On the other hand, how a subject is conditioned matters in terms of what pathways are involved in the placebogenic analgesia. If morphine is used, then an endogenous opioid mechanism is responsible for the placebogenic analgesia. However, if a nonopioid is used, then a different pathway is activated. The complexity of placebogenic analgesia that Amanzio and Benedetti identified (and which other researchers have since elaborated further) shows that the underlying mechanisms for placebo effects are varied and diverse.

2.4 Objective Measurements of Placebo Effects

It is a common belief that placebo effects only exist for "subjective" conditions such as pain, anxiety, nausea, concentration, and so on. Several recent studies, however, have led to a rethinking of this conventional belief. In 2018, a team of researchers headed by Julia Kirchhof wanted to see if conditioning-induced placebo effects can moderate immune responses.[23] That is, the study sought to demonstrate whether placebo might have distinctive physiological effects, and not "merely" psychological or phenomenological ones (granting, of course, that psychological effects are likely mediated by some physiological changes). Kirchhof's team recruited thirty renal transplant patients who were already taking immunosuppressants and they were briefed on the aims and the process of the experiment. On the first day, researchers measured subjects' T cell levels two, six, and ten hours after their morning regimen of immunosuppressants. On the second, third, and fourth day (the "acquisition" phase), the morning and evening rounds of immunosuppressants were accompanied by a novel green drink (a mixture of strawberry milk, lavender oil, and green food dye). Subjects then continued their regular two regimens of immunosuppressants for the next two days. On the seventh and eighth day (the "evocation" phase), subjects took their morning and evening immunosuppressants but, in addition, two placebo pills were sandwiched in during the day. All four pills were accompanied by the novel green drink (see Figure 2).

On the eighth and final day, Kirchhof et al., measured the subjects' T cell levels at the same intervals as on the first day. Unlike the initial measurements, in which T cell levels expectedly crept upward between the morning and evening regimens of immunosuppressants, the T cell levels on the eighth day (the second evocation day) *decreased* during the course of the day (see Figure 3). From a clinical point of view, the possible benefits are enormous. The side effects of

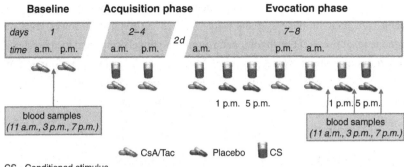

Figure 2 Structure of Kirchhof et al.'s study

Note: During baseline measures (day 1; without any drug-cue association), blood samples were taken at three different times: 2, 6, and 10 hours after morning (9 a.m.) drug intake. During the acquisition days 2–4, the immunosuppressive drug intake at 9 a.m. and 9 p.m. was combined with the conditioned stimulus (CS) (green-colored, new-tasting drink). During evocation days (study days 7 and 8), the morning and evening drug intake was again combined with the CS. In addition, patients received placebo pills at 4 hours (1 p.m.), as well as 8 hours (5 p.m.), together with the CS. At the second evocation day, blood samples were taken three times: 2, 6, and 10 hours after morning drug intake (9 a.m.).

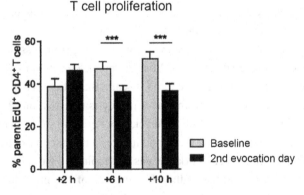

Figure 3 Comparison of T cell levels taken on the first day and the eighth day

immunosuppressants are notoriously unpleasant for patients. If a suppression of T cell production can be achieved with the use of placebos, health management after organ transplantations, for instance, would be far less challenging.

For our purpose, Kirchhof et al.'s study forces us to reconsider the belief that placebogenic effects are largely subjective. Here, T cell counts can be quantified, and are not the sort of things that one ought to be able to modify and assess by reflection alone. Moreover, the participants were told of the exact nature of the trial; they knew they were drinking a neutral concoction accompanied by placebos. Yet, their immune systems were "nudged" to maintain a lower level of immune response as if the conditioned stimuli (the novel drinks and the placebos) were reminders of the "correct" level of T cells. The conclusion, therefore, is that placebo effects cannot be dismissed as subjective patient reports that are susceptible to biases and difficult to compare across different individuals.

2.5 Placebo Surgeries Can Improve Mobility

Measurable placebo effects are not limited to our immune systems. A series of studies shows that placebo surgeries in which no surgical manipulations are made can provide lasting mobility improvement in patients suffering from musculoskeletal injuries.

One of the most common forms of back fracture is osteoporotic vertebral compression fractures. As we age, bones lose density and become more fragile, which in turn increases the risk of fracture. A nasty fall can fracture one's spine resulting in excruciating pain, a significant loss of mobility, and possible damage to spinal nerves. Vertebral compression fractures are a particular kind of facture in which a crack on one side of a vertebra causes the bone to collapse on itself. Because of the vertical pressure exerted on the damaged vertebra, patients with vertebral compression fractures can only find relief from their pain when they lie on their backs. Of course, this renders them bedridden, unable to perform any tasks that involve the use of their spines.

Vertebroplasty is a standard treatment for vertebral compression fractures and the basic idea is fairly intuitive. After the precise location of the fracture has been identified with imaging (e.g., a CT scan), the patient is placed on their stomach and receives local anesthesia. A needle is inserted into the fracture and organic cement injected to fill the crack (see Figure 4). If the compression is too severe, the surgeon first inserts and inflates a balloon to expand the gap before filling it with the cement (known as kyphoplasty). Numerous noncontrolled studies have established the effectiveness of the procedure. In one study, for instance, patients experienced a 60 percent decrease in pain, a 29 percent improvement in physical functioning, and a 29 percent decrease in hospitalization.[24]

The wide acceptance of vertebroplasty as an effective treatment for vertebral fractures did not, however, quell all concerns. As the number of vertebroplasties performed reached its apex in 2008, there was still no randomized controlled trial confirming its efficacy. Daniel Kallmes – a neurological surgeon at the Mayo Clinic in Rochester, Minnesota – noticed that clinicians would occasionally inject the cement into the wrong vertebra. More amazingly, these patients

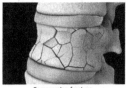

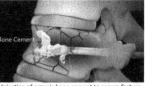

Compression fracture   Insertion of trocars via the patient's back   Injection of organic bone cement to secure facture

Figure 4 An illustration of vertebroplasty in which organic cement is injected into the site of the fracture

Note: Courtesty of SMART Imagebase, October 31, 2022. https://ebsco.smartimagebase .com/vertebroplasty-and-kyphoplasty/view-item?ItemID=77260.

reported comparable positive results. Kallmes led a team of researchers to compare the effectiveness of vertebroplasty against a sham equivalent across eleven study centers in the United States, United Kingdom, and Australia.[25] A total of 131 patients enrolled in the randomized study. After patients had been properly prepped, the surgeon hit a key on the computer that told them whether the patient was in the active or control arm. If the former, they proceeded as usual. If the latter, the surgeon opened the cement to simulate the smell of the injection (it smells of nail polish remover) and pressed on the back of the patient as they would with vertebroplasty. No injection was made and the patients in both arms rested an hour or two before being discharged.

The results showed that patients in both the active and the control arms had comparable improvements as measured by a mobility survey and self-reported pain. In terms of back-related disability, both groups experienced similar gain three days after the intervention that lasted for a month. The subjects in the control arm of Kallmes et al.'s trial experienced significant mobility improve-ments while the vertebral fractures remained untreated. Compression fractures not only cause severe pain, they can also compromise the musculoskeletal integrity of the spine. Patients with untreated vertebral compression fractures should not be able to return to normal physical functionality. One subject, "Bonnie," stated in an BBC interview that she was able to return to playing golf almost daily seven days after the vertebroplasty trial even though she received the sham procedure.[26]

As a result of Kallmes et al.'s study, the number of vertebroplasties performed has gradually declined since 2008. It is natural to conclude that the medical community responded exactly as one would hope: if a procedure does not outperform its sham equivalence, we should stop performing it. After all, the very concept of *clinical effectiveness* is defined as the difference between the outcome of the active arm and the control arm: no difference means no effectiveness as intended by the treatment.

If we focus on patients' experience, however, it might be worth reconsidering whether we should stop performing vertebroplasty. The fact remains that vertebroplasty brings significant benefits to patients; that it does not outperform sham vertebroplasty does not mean that it is useless. Imagine if someone is experiencing significant pain from a vertebral compression fracture and they learn that vertebroplasty can alleviate the pain; the fact that its therapeutic benefits are placebogenic matters little. Currently, there is no formal mechanism to introduce sham surgeries into clinical practice. Until we know what aspects of vertebroplasty are therapeutically irrelevant, the entire package remains an effective treatment option.

One of the most compelling characteristics of vertebroplasty is how commonsensical it seems. A patient fractures their back and experiences severe pain and limited mobility. From a causal point of view, if the fracture causes the pain, then the elimination of the fracture ought to improve the patient's condition. Like a crack in the foundation of a house, by cementing the fractured vertebra back together to restore structural integrity, surely it would help restore functionality and lessen discomfort? Anecdotal accounts clearly confirm this intuitive picture. Many of the examples of placebogenic effects share this characteristic; that is, the procedure has a clear and compelling narrative. In Section 3, I will argue that these narratives are causally important in the generation of placebo effects.

2.6 Debunking Placebo Effects

In a series of exhaustive meta-analyses culminating in their 2010 publication, Asbjørn Hróbjartsson and Peter Gøtzsche pooled together all published clinical trials that included a placebo-controlled arm along with a no-treatment arm to assess the presence of placebo effects.[27] The 2010 meta-analysis contained 202 trials with more than 15,000 subjects covering 60 clinical conditions. These included anxiety, pain, smoking cessation, hypertension, depression, asthma, dementia, vomiting, and nausea. Although Hróbjartsson and Gøtzsche had concluded in their earlier and more limited analyses that they "found no evidence of a generally large effect of placebo interventions" and that the small effect in patient-reported studies could be a product of bias,[28] their 2010 analysis drew a more measured and nuanced conclusion. They wrote:

> [O]ur findings do not imply that placebo interventions have no effect. We found an effect on patient-reported outcomes, especially on pain. Several trials of low risk of bias reported large effects of placebo on pain, but other similar trials reported negligible effect of placebo, indicating the importance

of background factors . . . . So, despite a general picture of low effects, and the risk of response bias and small sample size bias, it is likely that large effects of placebo interventions may occur in certain situations.[29]

A weak interpretation of Hróbjartsson and Gøtzsche's conclusion is that placebo effects might be of therapeutic interest for certain clinical conditions such as pain. A strong interpretation might be that we cannot rule out the presence of placebo effects for some clinical conditions without larger studies that can minimize some of the biases that placebo studies invariably contain (e.g., the inability to maintain double-blinding).

In some respects, Hróbjartsson and Gøtzsche's conclusion that, when pooled together, clinical trials seem to provide little evidence for placebo effects is unsurprising. One reason is that placebo effects might exist within specific contexts for specific conditions. Being in a healing context such as seeking care at a clinic is a major contributor to placebo effects. Diverse contexts can mean inconsistent results. Moreover, placebo effects only reside within a narrow set of physiological conditions (a phenomenon that we will examine more closely in the next section). The unrestricted inclusion of physiological conditions might drown out robust placebo effects in isolated trials.

Another reason to resist Hróbjartsson and Gøtzsche's conclusion is that the inclusion criteria they used were problematic. Only clinical trials that had a placebo-controlled arm were included. To screen potential trials, they merely relied on the declaration of the original researchers; that is, if a researcher said their experiment contained a placebo-controlled arm, then Hróbjartsson and Gøtzsche accepted it at face value. Given the murkiness of what exactly constitutes a placebo control, relying on the judgments of the original researchers might lead to the inclusion of dubious trials.

Take Kimberley Foster et al.'s 2004 investigation into the therapeutic benefits of the Trager approach in treating chronic headaches, which was included among Hróbjartsson and Gøtzsche's cohort.[30] Foster et al.'s study had three arms: an active arm consisting of the Trager approach (a physical manipulation treatment combined with relaxation training); a placebo-controlled arm consisting of weekly 15–20 minute meetings between patients and physicians and physical examinations; and a no-treatment arm. Did the meetings and physical examinations in the control arm qualify as proper placebos? These meetings are placebos so long as they provided everything that the Trager approach did, short of the studied intervention. Sham Trager would qualify as an adequate control, which Foster et al. did not consider. The meetings between the physicians and the patients in the control arm were entirely different from the experience patients received in the active arm, and this seems to cast doubts that Foster et al. had a proper placebo control.

The ideal method by which we can ascertain the power of placebos is to conduct clinical trials pitting a placebo (active) arm against a no-treatment arm. Alas, there have been only a handful of published experiments of this sort; thirty-two in total, by my count. Although Hróbjartsson and Gøtzsche were able to identify over 200 trials with a placebo-controlled arm and a no-treatment arm, the vast majority of these did not aim to study the therapeutic power of placebo per se. Instead, the placebo-controlled arm existed as a comparison to the active arm to determine the therapeutic effectiveness of some experimental treatment. The existence and extent of experimental biases is well known. When researchers have an incentive to demonstrate the effectiveness of the experimental treatment, there exists a motivation to obtain high positive outcomes in the active arm and low outcomes in the control arm. And, if a placebo-controlled arm is compared to a no-treatment arm (as in these studies), we would naturally see a perverse incentive to minimize the differences between the two. To put it plainly, the inclusion of a placebo-controlled arm in a clinical trial that aims to study some other active intervention entails an incentive to minimize placebogenic effects.

For some researchers, Hróbjartsson and Gøtzsche's studies offer evidence that placebo effects do not exist. A closer examination, however, shows that this conclusion is not warranted. Placebo effects might very well exist for specific conditions under specific circumstances. By lumping all placebo-controlled trials together, Hróbjartsson and Gøtzsche risk overwhelming the signals with noise. Furthermore, some of their methodological decisions (such as inclusion criteria) undercut the fidelity of their analysis. In light of the fact that their meta-analyses have been tremendously influential, it behooves us to be aware of their limitations.

2.7 Labels, Sizes, and Colors Can Affect the Magnitude of Placebo Effects

The seemingly secondary characteristics of an intervention such as its color, physical size, and the way it is labeled can affect its placebogenic power. A study by Slavenka Kam-Hansen et al., for example, shows how a drug's label might alter its therapeutic effectiveness.[31] A cohort of sixty-six subjects documented untreated migraine attacks. For six attacks, they randomly received one of the combinations in the table below, either a rizatriptan pill (Maxalt, a triptan-class drug that is used to treat migraines) or a placebo pill. Each of the six pills was labeled once as "Maxalt" or "Placebo" or "Maxalt or Placebo."

Maxalt labeled as "Maxalt"	Maxalt labeled as "Placebo"	Maxalt labeled as "Maxalt or Placebo"
Placebo labeled as "Maxalt"	Placebo labeled as "Placebo"	Placebo labeled as "Maxalt or Placebo"

In terms of their effectiveness in controlling migraine pain, placebo pills significantly outperformed no treatment. In addition, although Maxalt generally outperformed placebos regardless of labels, placebos labeled as "Maxalt" performed as well as Maxalt labeled as "Placebo." More oddly, Maxalt labeled as "Placebo or Maxalt" outperformed Maxalt labeled as "Maxalt." Somehow, the uncertainty of whether one had ingested a placebo or Maxalt rendered the Maxalt pills more effective. In addition to labeling, the color of a pill can alter its efficacy. In a 1996 study, Anton de Craen et al. showed that subjects tended to associate stimulants with red, yellow, and orange and depressants with blue and green.[32] In terms of actual efficacy, those who ingested blue placebos reported being more drowsy and less alert. Interestingly, in an Italian review, male subjects preferred orange color tranquilizers and female subjects preferred blue ones.[33] Similar results have been observed by other researchers.[34] One possible explanation for why Italian men do not prefer blue sedatives is that blue is the color of their national football team. Years of heartaches and thrills may have left many male fans traumatized by the color blue.[35] Other incidental features such as price points,[36] generic versus brand-named,[37] and even size of the pill and whether it is a capsule or a tablet can influence a drug's efficacy.[38]

What these studies show is that incidental features can contribute to the therapeutic benefits of a treatment. According to the orthodox view, a treatment contains two components: characteristic features that define what the treatment is and incidental features that accompany the treatment. As we will see in Section 4, we can think of placebo effects as those that are caused by incidental features. If we can reliably elicit placebogenic benefits via incidental features, we ought to question whether the line between characteristic and incidental features is justified. This in turn pushes us to question where we should draw the boundaries of any treatment. Not only would this be a philosophically important task, it can also impact medical practice, from determining what insurance should cover to how novel treatments are to be tested.

3 Mechanisms of Placebo Effects

3.1 An Evolutionary Story

Placebo effects are not magic; instead, they are real physical phenomena that obey the laws of physiology and physics. And, as such, if we understand the causal mechanisms involved, we should be able to induce them consistently on a par with other physiological responses.

As with any organic behaviors, there ought to be an evolutionary account for the emergence of placebo effects that shows how they are conducive to survival and reproduction. A number of scholars have offered the hypothesis that placebo effects are our body's responses to the presence of a safe environment for healing. For instance, Leander Steinkopf argues that pain, nausea, and other immune system responses are signals our body sends to indicate that we are in distress and need help.[39] Once certain we are safe (e.g., in the company of other individuals who can ensure our security), we can begin self-repair or healing. Warning signals like pain have fulfilled their functions and they are no longer needed. The endogenous opioid system, for instance, begins to produce analgesics to lessen the pain; that is, to turn off the alerting signals.

Placebo responses, according to this line of thinking, are a part of a complex physiological system that assesses the danger surrounding an individual and determines when it is safe to allocate precious resources to initiate the healing process. The presence of a caring physician, ingesting medicine, and a gentle touch tell our body that we are no longer under immediate threat and can safely begin recovery. If this hypothesis is correct, it would nicely explain why we only find placebo effects for specific physical experiences; pain, nausea, and other immediate reactions serve to alert us that we have been injured. Placebo analgesia generated by the expectation of pain relief taps into this mechanism by convincing the body that we are aware of the injury and that the pain signal is no longer necessary. This evolutionary account also provides a compelling explanation for why healers, from revered shamans to allopathic doctors, can be found in just about every culture prior to the advent of effective medical treatments.[40] Healers provide a deluge of cues to the body that the injury is being attended to and that the signals can cease. Perhaps it is from this relationship between the body's distress signals and healers' ability to cue the body into turning them off that the practice of medicine emerged.

With regard to the physiological mechanisms responsible for placebo effects, there are three main candidates: (1) classical conditioning, (2) expectancy, and (3) the Bayesian brain model. Although these three theories overlap in certain areas, they are distinct enough to deserve separate treatments.

3.2 Placebo Effect as Conditioned Response

Like many undergraduates, I learned about classical conditioning in an introductory course in psychology. But it was while caring for my mother that I realized how powerful and rapidly acquired conditioned responses could be.

As she was battling stomach cancer, a feeding tube was necessary to ensure adequate nutrition. Because of the location and extent of the tumor mass, the placement of a larger and more conventional gastric feeding tube was impossible. The surgeon thus suggested the placement of a small tube into her jejunum (the first segment of small intestines attached to the stomach). Its minute size along with the challenging placement meant that the tube could be dislodged easily. Meanwhile, it was urgent that my mother received a substantial amount of calories since she was severely underweight. With a high infusion rate of liquid nutrient via a small feeding tube, however, came the risk of spillage at the site of the graft. One evening, after the staff had increased the pump's infusion rate, a small quantity of nutrient leaked onto her still open surgical wound. The pain must have been excruciating. My mother woke up screaming in pain.

From that point on, whenever the pump reached the same rate, she would experience acute pain even if no nutrient was in contact with her incision. I tried mightily to explain to her that the difference between 24 ml/hour and 25 ml/hour was practically negligible. Yet, she was convinced that 25 ml/hour was too aggressive; the pain was a sign that her intestines "just couldn't take it." Given the urgency of achieving a high rate of infusion, I took the liberty one evening of turning the pump's digital display away from her. I also surreptitiously increased the infusion rate (being her healthcare proxy, I felt I was in the clear ethically). It was not until the pump reached 50 ml/hour that I revealed what I had done. My mother was mildly annoyed by my trickery. The fact that she was wrong about her intestines' ability to tolerate a high infusion probably caused greater upset. Although the pairing of pain with 25 ml/hour occurred only once, it sufficed to elicit extreme pain whenever the pump displayed "25 ml." And, as quickly as the fog of the conditioned pain came, it immediately dissipated in the face of contrary evidence.

Classical conditioning explains learned behaviors by associating a neutral stimulus (conditioned stimulus or CS) with another stimulus (unconditioned stimulus) that elicits a reflexive response (unconditioned response). Once the CS is sufficiently paired with the reflexive response such that it alone can elicit the response, the latter becomes the conditioned response. For instance, Pavlov's dog is presented with food (unconditioned stimulus) along with the ringing of a bell (CS).[41] The sight and smell of the food causes the dog to salivate instinctively (unconditioned response). After a sufficient period of pairing between the bell and the food, the dog begins to salivate when the bell is rung, regardless of the presence of food. The salivation then becomes the conditioned response to the CS of the ringing of the bell.

The idea that placebo effects, at least a subset of them, are the results of classical conditioning has enjoyed widespread acceptance. One of the earliest experiments on placebo effects by Richard Herrnstein involved repeated injections of scopolamine (an anti-nausea medication) in rats that depressed their appetite. When Herrnstein substituted saline for the scopolamine, the rats behaved similarly. He thus concluded that the saline-induced response "may reasonably be termed a placebo effect .... . [T]he manner in which it was brought about suggest[s], moreover, that it is an example of Pavlovian conditioning."[42] Similarly, in the immunosuppressant study conducted by Julia Kirchhof et al., cited in Section 2.4, subjects were placed in an "acquisition phase" in which immunosuppressants were paired with a novel drink. In the "evocation" phase, Kirchhof et al. measured T cell concentrations after subjects had ingested the novel drink alone and placebo pills. The low level of T cells, Kirchhof et al. argued, was a placebo response that relied on the earlier conditioned association of the unfamiliar drink and depressed T cell counts. The view that some placebo effects are nothing more than specific instances of classical conditioning is so common that placebo researchers routinely use it to induce placebo effects in placebo experiments.

However well-regarded the placebo-effect-as-conditioned-response view is, there are some basic problems which show that it provides, at best, an incomplete account of placebo effects. First, numerous clinical trials have shown that placebo effects can emerge without any prior conditioning. As we will discuss shortly, expectancy is an alternative account that explains placebo effects in terms of subjects' expectation of certain experiences. The idea that expectations can change a patient's response to an intervention is nothing new. Proponents of the classical conditioning theory of placebo effects are aware of these apparent counterexamples. Most moderate their views by claiming that classical conditioning provides a partial, albeit central, account of placebo effects.

However, two additional worries raise deeper conceptual troubles for the theory. Researchers often cite Pavlov's classic salivating-dog experiment in their introduction to the conditioning theory of placebo effects. Although the example nicely illustrates the key concepts in classical conditioning, it is certainly odd to think of salivation as a placebo response. There are numerous conditioned responses that do not appear to be placebogenic. Suppose my dog becomes excited when I pick up the leash because I always attach the leash when I take her on a walk. My dog's excitement is clearly a classically conditioned response but we would not call the excitement a placebo effect. If classical conditioning is to be an analysis of placebo effects, it ought to provide an account of why some conditioned responses are placebogenic while some are not.

Many proponents of the classical conditioning theory of placebo effects believe they are offering an analysis of the placebo effects; that is, some placebo effects are nothing more than special instances of classical conditioning. Moreover, a placebo is just the object that causally initiated the placebo effect. Recall that conditioning-induced placebo effects essentially piggyback on a causal connection between the unconditioned stimulus and the unconditioned response. I take a red-colored sleeping pill every day to fall asleep. The pharmacological agents in the pill slow my brain's activities and allow me to fall asleep more easily. When I take a dummy red pill to trigger the same decrease in brain activities, it relies on the nonpharmacological features of the nightly taking of the sleep aid to initiate the placebogenic process. That is, the dummy red pill works by exploiting all the nonpharmacological features that accompany my nightly taking of the sleeping pills, such as the drinking of a glass of water, the color of the pill, and the swallowing.

The terms "pharmacological agent" and "nonpharmacological agents" are supposed to distinguish placebo effects from nonplacebo effects. Effects caused by pharmacological agents are not placebogenic. The fact that I fall asleep after taking a sleeping pill is not a placebo effect if I fall asleep as the causal result of the pharmacological agent. In contrast, effects caused by the nonpharmacological agent qualify as placebo effects. If the act of swallowing a dummy red pill causes me to slow my brain activities, then the effect is placebogenic. Scholars have also used "specific" and "nonspecific" actions to draw a similar distinction, with the former corresponding to the effects caused by the pharmacological agent and the latter to those not caused by the pharmacological agent.

The specific/nonspecific distinction is notoriously difficult to define. And, without something like it, it would be impossible to say whether an effect is placebogenic. Put differently, it is necessary to know whether the specific or the nonspecific part of a treatment caused an effect in order to determine if the effect is placebogenic. The problem is that unless we can tell independently what part of an intervention is specific and what part nonspecific, it is not possible to tell if an effect is a placebo effect. Classical conditioning can, at best, tell us that *if* an effect is placebogenic, then it is the result of classical conditioning; it cannot tell us whether the effect is placebogenic. To answer the latter question, we would need to know what constitutes the specific and the nonspecific parts of a treatment – a topic we will tackle in Section 4. The conditioning view can tell us that, for some placebo effects, the underlying physiological mechanism is classical conditioning. It cannot tell us whether the initial effects are placebogenic. In this respect, it is not an analysis of placebo effects in the sense that it tells us the necessary and sufficient conditions for placebo effects.

3.3 Placebo Effect as the Result of Expectation

The fact that numerous clinical trials show that placebo effects can emerge without any prior conditioning strongly suggests that classical conditioning represents just one possible mechanism for placebo effects. Take the series of five German studies that show sham acupuncture is as effective as the *verum* counterpart. In three of the trials,[43] the researchers excluded candidates who had had acupuncture treatments within the previous twelve months. Nonetheless, many of the participants in the placebo groups had significant improvements in comparison to the no-treatment groups.

Like the conditioning view, the expectancy view must also contend with the abundance of counterexamples in which placebo effects seem to arise without any expectation on the part of the subjects. In addition to the plethora of clinical trials in which conditioning managed to elicit placebo effects without the presence of overt expectations, posttrial qualitative studies also indicate that placebo effects can occur when patients have no expectation of the intervention's efficacy. Nested within their broader trial on the therapeutic benefits of placebo acupuncture on IBS, Ted Kaptchuk's team interviewed 27 of the 262 subjects at the outset, midpoint, and conclusion of the trial regarding subjects' expectations.[44] Almost all the interviewed subjects expressed that they had no expectation that the intervention would improve their condition, although many hoped that it would. The fact that subjects had had no prior experience with acupuncture and that they were overwhelmingly unsure of the therapeutic efficacy of acupuncture strongly imply that their lack of expectation was genuine, if not well justified.

Other studies have shown that the magnitude of placebo effects is not linear or even monotonic with respect to subjects' degree of expectation. In a study on placebo-induced dopamine release among Parkinson's disease patients, subjects were told that they would have a 25 percent, 50 percent, 75 percent, or 100 percent chance of receiving levodopa – a first-line pharmacological treatment for Parkinson's-related motor impairment.[45] In reality, all the subjects received placebos. The results of the trial showed statistically significant placebo-induced improvement only for subjects in the 75 percent group. The 100 percent group performed worse than the other three groups.

Finally, the concept of *expectancy* is often left vaguely defined in placebo trials. From the point of view of ordinary usage, "expectancy" does not merely refer to any subjective credence greater than zero. If I bought a lottery ticket, it would be odd to say that I expect to win. As Kaptchuk et al. noted, expectancy is also not the same as hope.[46] I can hope that I win the lottery and not expect to win, and I might expect to die but not hope that it happens. Without a sharper understanding of expectancy, especially as defined clearly to trial participants, experiments that attempt to ascertain the relationship between expectancy and placebo effects might not be measuring the right thing.

3.4 The Bayesian Brain Model[+]

Both classical conditioning and expectancy views treat the brain as a passive organ reacting to unadulterated stimuli. Recently, advocates of the Bayesian brain model (BBM) have suggested that placebo effects are not just passive physiological reactions; instead, a person's background beliefs sort and shape incoming stimuli that cause their body to respond accordingly, blurring the line between what is happening and what is experienced.

Drawing on the principles of Bayesian probability, proponents of the Bayesian brain argue that our brain updates beliefs in accordance with the well-known Bayes' theorem. More importantly, the model tells us that when we are updating beliefs, we must make sense of the incoming stimulus by assigning to it a probability. When we see something that looks like a snake, how likely is it that it is actually a snake? Here, prior beliefs about the contextual cues (e.g., I am in my apartment) and knowledge about snakes (e.g., urban apartments are not the normal habitat for snakes) help us assess the likelihood that there is in fact a snake, as opposed to a toy, a cucumber, or a cat's tail. This practice of guessing the nature of our observations is known as predictive coding and it is indispensable to how we make sense of the world around us. As Jeff Hawkins and Sandra Blakeslee write, "As strange as it sounds, when your own behavior is involved, your predictions not only precede sensation, they determine sensation."[47] In other words, observations or stimuli do not come to us as raw data; instead, they are sorted and shaped by our prior beliefs. The revisions can take place entirely unconsciously.

When incoming stimuli prove difficult to reconcile with our other beliefs, the Bayesian brain revises along the path of least resistance. Our brain creates a narrative that minimizes the rejection of strongly held beliefs, including our observations. When I am in a woodsy area known to have snakes, I am much more likely to construe a fast-slithering object as a snake than I am when relaxing in my urban apartment. The BBM explains this on the grounds that an observation of a snake fits much better with my beliefs when I am in a woodsy area than when I am in my apartment. I am far more likely to construe the slithering observation *as a snake* in a woodsy area than in my apartment. The BBM tells us that we literally see things differently, depending on our background beliefs.

A personal experience shows vividly how our brain actively shapes what we observe. At the Ashton Graybiel Spatial Orientation Laboratory at Brandeis University, one of the main research foci is the brain's ability to orient us in a zero-gravity environment. Contrary to depictions in popular media, floating around without gravity is a tremendously disorienting and potentially debilitating experience. Imagine that you are spinning backward in a space station. Your visual cues tell you that you are moving backward while the feedback from your moving legs signal that you are walking forward. At the same time, your vestibular system is giving you additional conflicting data. In order to restore harmony, your brain attempts to tell a story that might include ignoring some stimuli, warping other observations, or rejecting some (prior) beliefs. If your brain fails to reconcile them, it sends a signal to your digestive system that you must vomit. How else can you explain what you are experiencing unless you have eaten something poisonous?

An instrument – the optokinetic drum – investigates what happens when our visual and motorsensory inputs conflict (see Figure 5). The apparatus is an enclosed vertical cylinder with black and white stripes lining the interior. The wall of the cylinder, the handlebar, and the floor can move at independent rates. Once the door is closed, subjects have no external sensory cues. Suppose the wall is being spun at 20 rpm and the floor and handlebar are moving at 10 rpm (much like the sensory experience of someone falling forward in space). How does our brain make sense of the dissonance?

Because a close friend, Ely Rabin, was a researcher at the lab, I spent far too many hours as Ely's first-line research subject. When placed in the scenario

Figure 5 The optokinetic drum

Note: Courtesy of the Graybiel Spatial Orientation Laboratory.

described above, the illusion I experienced was overwhelming and shocking. And it occurred even though I was told what I could experience before stepping into the drum. As the wall and floor began to move, the firm vertical wall of the cylinder began to collapse toward me. Of course, no contact was made, so at the very last second, the wall would quickly pull back, reset, and begin to collapse again and again. Other subjects report suddenly seeing their legs elongated to twice their normal length and some (unfortunate) subjects experience nothing at all. The optokinetic drum provides a tremendously powerful experience of our Bayesian brain at work: it weaves together a story to minimize disruption between our unique sets of prior beliefs and incoming stimuli. If our brain needs to fabricate an incredible lie to make it fit, so be it.

The BBM tells us that placebogenic experiences are results of our brain doing a particular kind of updating. Consider the classic placebo analgesic cream experiment. Clinicians induce painful stimulations in subjects. They then tell them that an analgesic cream (a placebo, in reality) will lessen the pain while a hidden IV line injects an actual analgesic. Once properly conditioned, subjects then receive the cream without the surreptitious analgesic but they experience less pain, nonetheless. The BBM would explain the analgesic experience as the result of our brain making sense of incoming stimuli: clinics are where we usually experience reduced discomfort, clinicians tell me I am receiving a painkiller, the cream has worked recently, etc. The subject's brain predicts that they will experience less pain and it delivers that result by ignoring the lack of analgesia in the cream and releasing endogenous opioid instead. The prediction is confirmed and the web of beliefs restores coherence.

Revisions of beliefs and sensory experiences are guided by the goal of maintaining coherence, according to the BBM. Classical conditioning can play an important role insofar as some beliefs might be the results of prior conditioning. The belief that a cream being applied is an analgesic, for instance, can come from an earlier pairing between the cream and the hidden infusion of an analgesia. Likewise, expectancy can create beliefs about what will happen. When subjects are told that a cream is an analgesic, they might form the expectation that they will experience less pain. What distinguishes the BBM from the other two views of placebo mechanisms is that the BBM does not care how beliefs are formed; instead, it tells us that placebo effects are the results of our brain reconciling conflicts. The BBM can accommodate the counterexamples that plague both the conditioning view and the expectancy view.

The BBM has been confirmed by a handful of studies. A 2017 study by Won-Mo Jung et al., for instance, found significant correlation between their computational predictions of subjects' pain experience using a Bayesian model and actual subjects' reports from an analogous clinical trial.[48] In addition, the model also captures some of the more odd observations researchers have noticed in clinical trials. As we saw earlier, a greater assurance of the power of a placebo intervention does not always correspond to greater placebo effect. One explanation is that when subjects are told that the intervention provides a total alleviation of pain, the assurance becomes implausible or quickly disconfirmed by the presence of *any* painful sensations. Since, according to the theory, our brain is constantly updating with new evidence, the belief that an intervention is an extremely powerful analgesic becomes far less plausible when the subject feels pain. A more conservative or vague declaration about the power of an intervention provides more room for the brain to maintain the belief that the intervention has an analgesic property; in medicine and in the world at large, nothing is guaranteed.

Similarly, the BBM can also explain why placebo responses seem to cluster around certain physiological reactions. For instance, pain is one of the most common domains of placebo effects. The BBM can account for it in that the experience of pain can be modulated by a number of internal actions directed by our nervous system. From endogenous opioid to switching conscious attention away from the pain, the brain possesses many ways to turn off/down the pain dial. The same cannot be said for the production of insulin for those suffering from type 1 diabetes. Without a functioning pancreas (primarily, beta cells), no amount of placebo can increase insulin production. The fact that the body and nervous system are incapable of producing insulin without beta cells places a firm limit on what placebos can do with respect to patients with type 1 diabetes. The degree of involvement the brain has in a physiological function is thus correlated with the likelihood of placebo effects: the more the brain can affect a function, the more likely we are to find placebo effects. In addition, the brain plays an important part in maintaining homeostasis, but it is not a miracle worker. However much the Bayesian brain attempts to alter physiological functions to restore cognitive coherence, it cannot transcend the physiological limits of our organs.

The evolutionary account of placebo effects sketched at the start of this section fits nicely with the BBM. Scholars have argued that the cues from a healing environment can increase the magnitude of placebo effects. The BBM explains how these factors contribute to placebo effects. When in the company of a caring and competent healer who is offering treatments widely taken as effective, either these beliefs are false or I do, in fact, feel better. The more I believe I am in a safe place and my injury is being treated by individuals who want to make me feel better, the more likely my brain will lessen my discomfort. Revisions along the path of least resistance might provide enough pressure to bring about a real sense of improvement.

Replication of clinical results in placebo research is notoriously difficult. A small change in the experimental setup can lead to substantial changes in outcomes. Given the complex sets of prior beliefs we hold, it is not surprising that the results of our Bayesian revisions can vary radically. Someone who has little confidence in the efficacy of Western medicine might respond very differently to a placebo than a similar patient with a higher degree of faith. Unless we can control for *all* the salient beliefs that are at play in a revision, we might not be able to say with confidence whether a placebo response will occur or not.

The power of the BBM to explain placebo effects is both its strength and its weakness. As Iñigo Arandia and Ezequiel Di Paolo have argued, the model appears to be able to explain *any* clinical results.[49] Given that Bayesian updating is done unconsciously, if a particular prediction does not take place, the plethora of an individual's conscious and unconscious beliefs can supply countless excuses for the predictive failure. Although the worry that the BBM is not falsifiable troubles me less than it does Irving Kirsch,[50] its apparent ability to explain any observation might undermine its usefulness.

I will mention two final caveats before leaving the discussion of the BBM. Experimental psychology has long recognized that the strength of individuals' desires can induce certain subjective experiences. The connection between desires and placebo effects has also been observed. In a study published in the journal *Pain*, Lene Vase et al. noted that the stronger the desire for pain relief IBS patients expressed, the greater their placebogenic analgesic responses.[51] The contribution desires can make to placebo effects cannot be easily captured by the BBM. Standardly, Bayesian updating concerns beliefs and the respective probabilities assigned to them. Desires do not have probability values since they are neither true nor false. Some Bayesian scholars have offered various ways to reduce desires to beliefs, incorporating the former into a Bayesian revision model whose only guide is to minimize errors in predictions.[52] For instance, one method is to reinterpret S's desire for X as S's prediction in the realization of X. To minimize errors, S will act in such a way that X comes true. Whatever explanatory work "desire" does, the Bayesian model can accommodate it by relying only on predictions and beliefs, so claim the proponents.

Meanwhile, other researchers such as Daniel Yon, Cecilia Heyes, and Clare Press have called for caution in the reductive approach on the grounds that it does not naturally account for a number of psychological phenomena.[53] Individuals with obsessive–compulsive disorder, for instance, often know that obsessive rituals are causally pointless but they still possess a strong desire to perform them. If the strength of one's desire can bring about placebogenic effects without there being any obvious expectations that these effects will come about, we might have to rethink the BBM to accommodate desires and other attitudes.

Since the BBM involves the revisions of beliefs, one concern is that it precludes the possibility of placebo responses that are not caused by beliefs in the subject. As mentioned before, a trial by Karin Jensen et al. showed that conditioning-induced placebogenic analgesia could be induced with visual stimuli that were below subjects' conscious recognition of them.[54] Likewise, a number of OLP trials have included subjects who did not believe in the efficacy of the placebo; they nonetheless experienced placebo effects.

Consider a typical psychotherapeutic relationship. Suppose for a moment that, as some scholars have concluded, the therapeutic effect of psychotherapy is primarily placebogenic.[55] Moreover, suppose that sharing our thoughts and emotions in a safe environment with a caring person is integral to the therapy's effectiveness. Meetings between patients and therapists constitute precisely this therapeutic environment except for one thing: a therapist is not a caring friend. As much as a therapist might genuinely empathize and listen to a patient's worries, a professional line exists between the two. If a therapist were to cross the line and become a patient's friend, one would chastise them for being unprofessional. Psychotherapy works, one might argue, precisely because the therapist is not a friend. In a therapist–patient relationship, confidentiality is paramount, therapists strive not to be judgmental, and physical contact such as giving one another hugs is considered inappropriate. These are all factors that make psychotherapy different from ordinary friendship. To put it bluntly, psychotherapy depends on make-believe emotional intimacy. And, it works even if the patient is fully aware of the nature of the arrangement.

One possible explanation for the therapeutic benefits of psychotherapy is that it is a kind of placebo effect that is generated by going through the rituals of verbalizing one's emotions to a caring person. A patient might not believe that the therapist actually cares (at least not in the same way as a close friend) but the benefits arrive nonetheless. Perhaps the same can be said of the placebo effect of a healer's warm touch. A patient's placebo responses can be automatic without any robust beliefs about whether the healer really cares. Superficial tactile feedback might trigger health responses like a soda machine detecting the right size and weight of an inserted object. A slug that has the correct specifications will successfully trigger the mechanism. The great extent of our autonomic nervous system leaves plenty of room for stimulation shortcuts that can elicit physiological responses without their customary causes. A BBM qua revisions of beliefs would have a tough time accommodating these placebogenic processes that are cognitively thin.

Although these two observations raise some prima facie problems for the BBM, my sense is that the model can account for them with further modifications. Alternatively, perhaps placebo effects come in two varieties: those brought about by Bayesian revisions and those brought about via stimulation shortcuts that take advantage of our autonomic nervous system. To acknowledge the need for amending the BBM, I will add a plus symbol to label it as "Bayesian brain model$^+$."

3.5 Meaning Response

Taking a broader view of placebos, anthropologist Daniel Moerman has proposed the theory that placebo effects are the results of the body responding to external cues steeped in meaning imbued by social institutions. When a patient experiences less pain after the application of an otherwise inert cream, a cluster of social signals from the physician's white coat to the high fee contribute to the initiation of a decrease in pain. In this sense, the identification of a placebo with, say, a pill or a sham surgery, is mistaken, Moerman argues. Placebogenic responses are instead the products of a multitude of meaningful social cues that trigger physiological changes. Coined "meaning response," Moerman argues that his theory allows for an understanding of placebo effects that escape the problems of the conditioning and expectancy hypotheses.

Moerman's meaning response shares some of the virtues of the BBM$^+$. Since the Bayesian revision of a belief depends on the person's other beliefs, we would expect the presence of placebo effects to vary across communities which hold radically different beliefs.[56] Different fundamental beliefs can entail that a practice that is meaningful in one community might have no meaning in another.

One potential concern with the meaning response theory is that it might have a difficult time distinguishing placebogenic from nonplacebogenic effects. Consider Claire who visits her psychiatrist in the hope of bringing her depression under control. In addition to their regular meetings, her psychiatrist has also prescribed antidepressants. Unbeknownst to Claire, the antidepressants are of marginal benefit; however, the visits to her psychiatrist instill in her a sense of control over her mood. A major contributor to the benefits of these visits comes from the impressive diplomas that hang behind her doctor. The benefits that Claire enjoys are (at least partially) placebogenic.

In contrast, consider Margot who also suffers from depression. During her daily subway commute, she sees a poster advertising the therapeutic benefits of antidepressants. After talking to her psychiatrist, she begins to take antidepressants regularly and her mood becomes significantly better due to the pharmacological effects of the antidepressants. Margot's therapeutic improvement is nonplacebogenic. In both cases, Claire's and Margot's improvements arose out of some meaningful cues (impressive diplomas vs. an advertisement). What makes the former improvements placebogenic and the latter not? Social cues can clearly be important parts of the causal chain that leads to therapeutic improvement. Meaning response might be too conceptually coarse to delineate placebogenic outcomes from nonplacebogenic ones.

Still, there is a great deal we can learn from Moerman's observation that meaningful cues can greatly contribute to therapeutic effectiveness. The recognition that placebo effects and therapeutic improvements in general are partly caused by "extramedical" factors follows the path first charted by proponents of the social determinants of health. Poverty, access to clean water, availability of reliable transportation, racism, and an individual's feeling of fulfillment can all affect health outcomes. While social determinants of health tend to focus on population-level improvements, Moerman's meaning response theory focuses on the effects social cues have on an individual's well-being. And, just as clinicians, researchers, and policymakers have recognized the impact social determinants have on our health, Moerman's meaning response theory will likely be better appreciated in both medical research and clinical care.

3.6 Plausible Narratives and the Stigma of Placebo Effects

This review of the dominant views on placebo mechanisms highlights the importance of narratives in eliciting placebo effects and it offers a way to destigmatize placebos. In health humanities, the term "narrative" primarily refers to the subjective experiences of participants in healthcare. Patients' narratives, for instance, typically consist of autobiographical accounts of their experiences with ailments and care. My use of the term "narrative" has a slightly different but related meaning. In sum, placebo effects require the presence of a plausible narrative from the subject's point of view. For instance, a placebo cream can confer placebogenic analgesia only if the subject believes that the narrative of a cream lessening pain is plausible. The exact details of the narrative are not important; as long as the subject believes (with a sufficiently high degree of confidence) that the analgesic effect of the cream is plausible, placebogenic analgesia is possible. A plausible narrative is thus a critical (and perhaps necessary) condition for placebo effects, at least those that are mediated by beliefs.[57]

Among those who believe in a causal picture of the world, the plausible narrative would consist of a rough causal account. This can certainly vary from worldview to worldview. Perhaps one believes that divine interventions are possible; this person's worldview includes the possibility of A affecting B without there being any physical causal connections. A plausible narrative for them might include noncausal interventions such as distant intercessional prayers. Just as folk psychology from the philosophy of mind helps us to understand the behaviors of other intentional beings by attributing beliefs and desires to them, an analogous folk causality gives us a rough framework to make sense of why things happen.

Consider the vertebroplasty study in Section 2.5. What makes the treatment (and its sham equivalent) so effective is that the procedure has a gripping narrative. The narrative tells us that the loss of mobility and pain are caused by a fracture in one's spinal column. In our everyday lives, if a support beam is cracked the application of cement helps restore structural integrity. Vertebroplasty takes advantage of this mental picture. A fracture in my vertebra causes pain, and cement that seals the cracks must thus help eliminate discomfort. And, regardless of whether the narrative is true or not, the fact that a patient has this mental picture allows for placebogenic benefits.

The plausible narrative requirement captures the view that placebo effects are not magical; that is, they cannot violate the constraints of our folk causality. After all, what constitutes magic is merely the violation of the laws of nature. If a subject believes that there are no possible paths that can link an intervention to an outcome, it is unlikely that there would be a placebo effect. Indeed, one can think of the BBM^+ as an argument for the plausible narrative requirement. According to the model, individuals update their beliefs and shape their observations to restore internal consistency while minimizing the rejection of more firmly held beliefs. The narrative plausibility requirement is another way of saying that we update our beliefs by aiming to retain our fundamental metaphysical views of the universe.

The narrative plausibility theory helps us make sense of some odd trends in medicine. Although acupuncture has been available as a treatment modality in the United States since the 1950s, the acceptance of acupuncture by the public did not occur for another forty years. One possible hypothesis is that, during the interim, the idea that clinicians can modify *qi* and elicit therapeutic responses by inserting needles gained traction. As the public became more aware of the acupuncture narrative, the placebogenic benefits took hold, creating a feedback loop.

The plausible narrative requirement suggests that individuals who believe that the efficacy path of an intervention is plausible would have a better chance of experiencing placebo effects. For the use of OLPs, how clinicians disclose the efficacy of a placebo treatment is thus paramount. Overpromising, as we have seen, will quickly render the narrative implausible. At the same time, sharing a rough sketch of how OLPs work with patients might improve the chance of the treatment's effectiveness.[58]

Since the plausible narrative hypothesis requires that subjects believe in the plausibility of an intervention's therapeutic pathway, it implies that placebo effects can only occur for those capable of having beliefs. If it turns out to be the case that placebo effects can arise without beliefs, then the plausible narrative theory would be wrong, at least for this class of placebo effects.

The classical conditioning, expectancy, and BBM⁺ views are all ultimately about learned or novel beliefs and behaviors. What is learning but the acquisition of new behaviors or beliefs? Placebo effects are about getting our bodies to respond in a novel way. An inert cream is not supposed to lessen our pain but, with sufficient conditioning, our body learns to respond to it differently. The cream is still the same cream but we are not the same person.

Perhaps the stigma that has been attached to placebos stems from how easy it is for us to change. The fact that novel placebogenic behaviors can arise with minimal intention on our part adds to placebo's unsettling nature. We would like to believe that we are in firm control of our bodies and our minds. Placebo effects have shown the magnitude of our plasticity. After eons of evolution, we have developed remarkable automatic mechanisms that strive to protect us. To be sure, some of these mechanisms (e.g., ensuring blood flows to our vital organs at the expense of our limbs) can be counterproductive at times. But the lessons of evolution have kept us alive. Inducing placebo effects teaches us how our automatic systems function and showcases the internal resources we all possess. They are no more mysterious or threatening than vaccines, which likewise take advantage of our automatic ability to acquire new immune responses. It is our capacity to learn new behaviors and beliefs that ensures our survival. Rather than thinking of placebo effects as the result of being fooled, I would instead think of them as my body's incredible ability to take care of me.

4 Philosophical Implications of Placebos: From the Elusiveness of Placebos to the Challenge of Authenticity

4.1 How Not to Define Placebos

I have avoided offering a clear definition of *placebo* and *placebo effect* in the first three sections. The key reason is that any evaluation of a proposed definition of *placebo* ought to be measured against how the term is used in clinical and medical research. Both Section 2 and Section 3 provide a rich set of data points that we can use to judge the adequacy of any proposed placebo-related definitions.

Having a clear understanding of placebo is valuable for a number of reasons. First, the careful examination of a concept can help uncover hidden assumptions and erroneous beliefs. In clinical care, knowing what placebo effects are can help us determine if they should be part of a clinician's therapeutic toolbox. Healthcare providers such as health maintenance organizations have a greater duty to provide placebo interventions if they are considered treatments. In medical research, a clear definition of *placebo effects* can tell us the real therapeutic power of an active intervention. Moreover, it will help us design better clinical trials that accurately assess placebo effects by ensuring that we are using the right baseline benchmark in the form of a placebo control.

The difficulties scholars have encountered in defining placebo stem not from a want of trying or smarts. The messiness of the broader theories within which a specific medical therapy sits and the context-dependency of a salient cause are ultimately responsible for the failures. This is the main argument offered in the present section and I will present a definition of *placebo* and *placebo effect* in light of it. As a preview, I take placebo effects to be nonnegative effects generated by the incidental features of a treatment. Since the line between characteristic and incidental features is largely driven by pragmatic considerations, the line between placebo and nonplacebo effects inherits the same characteristics. If we look for an in-principle (or nonpragmatic) definition of *placebo* and *placebo effect*, we will likely remain disappointed.

As briefly mentioned in Section 1, one of the most common definitions of placebo is that it is "an inert substance that provokes perceived benefits, whereas the term nocebo is used when an inert substance causes perceived harm."[59] Defining placebo as an inert substance leads to some obvious problems. For a start, if placebos are inert, then by definition they cannot have causal power and, therefore, they cannot produce any effects, beneficial or otherwise. Moreover, defining placebo as an inert substance rules out the possibility that pharmacologically active drugs can serve in the role of a placebo control in clinical trials. Commonly referred to as "active placebos," researchers have often used active pharmacological agents as controls in clinical trials. One reason is to mimic the side effects of the *verum* treatments so that subjects cannot infer which arm of the trial they belong to by the presence of side effects. By ensuring that subjects in the control arm have similar risks of experiencing the side effects of the experimental treatment, researchers reduce the risks of subjects unblinding themselves.

Richard Thomson, for instance, conducted an investigation into the effectiveness of tricyclic antidepressants by pitting them against an atropine control. Atropine belongs to a class of involuntary nervous system blockers and it is used to treat low blood pressure and to limit salivation before surgeries.[60] Thomson chose atropine as a placebo control because he wanted to ensure that subjects in the control arm experience dry mouth – a common side effect of tricyclic antidepressants. The use of active placebos would be logically impossible if placebos were necessarily inert.

One might be tempted to draw a distinction between complete inertness (inert *tout court*) and inertness relative to a certain physical condition or experimental aim. For instance, although atropine is not inert *tout court*, it does not have any therapeutic effects relative to depression. As a control for a study on antidepressants, atropine is causally inert in terms of its effects on depression, even though it is not causally inert *tout court*. Perhaps we can similarly distinguish the active and inert components of any treatment along the same lines. For any treatment, component A consists of elements that have positive causal effects relative to an ailment X, while component B consists of elements that do not. Component B might be causally efficacious for something other than X but it is causally inert relative to X. Placebo effects would thus be effects caused by B – an element that is causally inert relative to X.

Consider a patient taking an antibiotic to clear up a nasty infection. There are parts of the drug that kill bacteria, for instance, by destroying their cell walls. There are also parts of the drug that serve as the vehicle through which the medication is delivered. For example, starch is not only useful as a binding agent in the manufacture of pills, it can also help facilitate the absorption of the medication. Starch is not inert but relative to the purpose of killing bacteria, it is not an active ingredient. Suppose in addition to eliminating the infection, the mere act of taking a starch pill lowers the patient's anxiety. One might say that, relative to this context, the drug's antibacterial effect is nonplacebogenic and its ability to lower the patient's anxiety is placebogenic.

The problem is that identifying placebo effects with the effects caused by relatively inert components of a treatment rules out a certain class of placebo effects. Consider the use of an IV analgesia, perhaps a morphine injection. The opioid molecules are clearly responsible for the analgesic effect and we can think of it as the "active" ingredient of the treatment. Suppose that the mere act of receiving an injection confers some analgesic effect as well. Is this a placebo effect? If we define a placebo effect as one that is brought about by elements of a treatment that are causally inert relative to some condition, then this would not qualify as placebogenic. In fact, we can a priori rule out the possibility that a treatment for X can generate positive placebo effects on X since placebo effects cannot affect X. This seems to conflict greatly with how researchers understand placebo effects. Beneficial sham vertebroplasty, for instance, would be impossible since the elements that led to the positive therapeutic results are not causally inert (relative to the condition) and thus they cannot be placebo elements.

Instead of relying on inertness, researchers have looked to "specific" and "nonspecific" action to help define placebo-related concepts, as we mentioned in passing in Section 1. Arthur Shapiro provided one of the earliest and most influential definitions of placebo, which explicitly relies on the concept of *specific action*. He writes:

> A *placebo* is defined as any therapeutic procedure (or that component of any therapeutic procedure) (1) which is given deliberately to have an effect, or (2) which unknowingly has an effect, on a patient, symptom, disease, or syndrome, but which is objectively without specific activity for the condition being treated . . . . A *placebo effect* is defined as the changes produced by placebos.[61]

The specific/nonspecific language continues to appear in academic publications. Winfried Häuser, Emil Hansen, and Paul Enck, for instance, tell us that the effects of every treatment "are divided into specific and non-specific. Specific effects are caused by the characteristic elements of the intervention. The non-specific effects of a treatment are called placebo effects when they are beneficial and nocebo effects when they are harmful."[62]

The desire to draw a distinction between specific and nonspecific actions is entirely reasonable. If we identify a placebo (or a placebo part of a treatment) by tracing nonspecific actions to their causal origins, then we would certainly need a way to tell which actions are nonspecific. Without some distinction between specific and nonspecific actions, it would be nigh impossible to locate placebos or placebic parts.

According to Shapiro, a placebo is that which causes a positive therapeutic effect that has no specific action. But, what exactly does "specific action" mean? We might try to explicate these key concepts in terms of how well we understand the underlying therapeutic mechanisms. The difficulty is that we lack precise knowledge of the therapeutic mechanisms of a great deal of conventional therapies. Take ibuprofen. Although it is a widely used NSAID analgesic, its exact pharmacokinetics are largely unknown. If knowledge of the underlying mechanism is what distinguishes specific and nonspecific action, then far too many conventional treatments would have nonspecific actions and thus be placebogenic.

One might rely instead on some notion of intentionality to distinguish specific from nonspecific actions. For example, a treatment's effect is nonspecific if it is not the intended effect of the patient or prescribing clinician. The color of a pill is not intended to have a therapeutic effect. If it does, then it is a nonspecific and thus placebo effect.

It should be obvious that defining placebo effects on the basis of intentions will not do. After all, patients and clinicians can intend to use an intervention incorrectly. If placebo effects or nonspecific effects are merely those that come about unintentionally, then a patient who recovered from an infection after unintentionally taking antibiotics would thus have had a placebo experience and the antibiotics would be a placebo.[63]

Perhaps one might attempt to relativize the specific effects of a treatment to the manufacturer's intention or the recommendations of professional organizations. This would address the problem we have just considered. The specific action of an aspirin, thus, is that it blocks the production of the lipid prostaglandins which are necessary for inflammation and pain. If a patient takes an aspirin for a headache, its specific action is the diminished production of prostaglandins. The patient's anxiety might also decrease because they took a pill and the act of doing so provides some placebogenic benefits. Regardless of the intention of the patient, the *real* specific effects of aspirin are what the manufacturers and professional medical organizations say they are.

A problem with defining placebo in the context of this broader relativization is that there are clearly usages of therapies that deviate from manufacturers' or professionals' intentions. Known as off-label usage, pharmaceuticals are regularly used for purposes not intended by manufacturers. The use of antidepressants in adolescents was widespread before manufacturers and professional organizations declared it was appropriate. If a drug works for an eighteen-year-old, so off-label reasoning goes, then surely it would work on a seventeen-and-a half-year-old.[64] Similarly, oncologists often recommend treatment protocols that do not strictly target the type of cancer a patient has (perhaps no clinical trials have demonstrated their effectiveness for the type of cancer in question). There are many good reasons why the off-label use of treatment is justifiable, from the lack of any other therapeutic options to the oncologist's clinical experience with the protocol. If nonspecific actions are those that arise from using a therapy for a purpose not intended by the manufacturers or professional organizations, then all off-label effects would be placebogenic.

Some scholars have tried to define placebo effects in term of their causal paths; that is, what physiological subsystems (e.g., nervous, skeletal, metabolic, and so on) are involved. Placebo effects, some argue, must arise through the psychology of the subject.[65] Given our earlier discussion on whether cognition is a necessary criterion for experiencing placebo effects, the focus on psychology is perhaps not entirely off base. Still, there are two immediate problems here. First, it implies that there is a difference between psychological and physical effects and this requires the adoption of some form of dualism. Second, plenty of conventional treatments aim to affect our health via our psychology. From talk therapy to mood stabilizers, the success of these treatments to improve, say, our dietary habits runs through our psychology – but surely one does not want to attribute the benefits of dietary changes to placebo effects? At best, the requirement that placebo effects go through our psychology is a necessary but not sufficient condition.

One might suggest that what distinguishes placebos from nonplacebos is that placebo effects are not sensitive to a wide range of substitutions while nonplacebo effects are. For example, the exact shape of a pill makes little difference in terms of its placebo effects. The same cannot be said for the effects of an antibiotic. As the chemistry of an antibiotic is modified, its antibacterial power can change or disappear abruptly. Placebos are more tolerant of changes, so to speak; they are less invariant than nonplacebos.

Whether this proposal is plausible depends on empirical investigations. As we saw, the color of a pill can affect a sedative's effectiveness. Meanwhile, a wholesale substitution of one chemical with another from the same class of drugs often makes little difference in terms of therapeutic effectiveness. Furthermore, to measure stability across substitutions, we need to specify what constitutes a substitution. There are countless ways to vary the color of a pill that are indistinguishable to the human eye. Does each of these count as a substitution? There are many ways to vary the length of a therapy session and the vast majority of them make no difference in terms of the session's effectiveness. What then qualifies as a substitution? We certainly do not want to say that a change counts as a legitimate substitution just in case the change leads to relevant specific effects. This would give us the trivially true definition that a specific effect (nonplacebic effect) is one caused by features of a treatment that are invariant with respect to causing specific effects. If we did not know what a specific effect is, using "specific effect" to define it will not gain any epistemic ground. Finally, there is a deeper question that deserves to be answered. Why should invariance matter? Even if we can address the technical issues described above, is drawing a distinction between specific and nonspecific effects in terms of invariance philosophically meaningful? We might be able to sort treatments into these two categories (i.e., some are more stable across substitutions than others) but the distinction is only worthwhile if it tells us something philosophically significant.

As we saw in Section 3, scholars such as Moerman have advocated the view that placebo effects are positive physiological responses to certain meaningful cues. These "meaning responses" do not have to come from any specific discrete objects such as a placebo pill; rather, contextual contributors like a clinician's diplomas or the warm demeanor of a care provider can cause therapeutic improvements. Similarly, Howard Brody has long argued that placebo effects are "a bodily change due to the symbolic effects of a treatment or treatment situation."[66] Although there is a great deal of wisdom in recognizing the effects contextual factors can play in healing, both views must ultimately confront a variation of the same problem of distinguishing specific from nonspecific actions. Take Brody's view. Imagine a patient who is particularly lax when following their doctor's treatment prescription. To improve compliance, the patient decides to carry around an inspiring quotation (e.g., "Compliance is self-care"). The little trick works and the patient does a better job adhering to the prescription and their ailment disappears. Is the quotation a symbol in Brody's sense? It seems odd to say that the patient's improvement caused by better compliance is placebogenic. What distinguishes symbol-genic improvements that are placebo effects from those that are not? Just as scholars must distinguish the effects of a pill in terms of specific and nonspecific actions, Brody and Moerman must tell us what makes a feature of a treatment a contextual factor without begging the question.

4.2 From Defining *Placebos* to Defining *Treatments*

Although the attempts at delineation discussed in the previous subsection prove to be inadequate, the motivation behind drawing a distinction between two classes of features for any treatment such that one class consists of therapeutically relevant ones while the other does not is important. This is especially true if we are to define *placebo effects* as those produced by the nontherapeutic parts of a treatment such as the shape of a pill.

At the most abstract level, nonplacebo effects are the causal effects of some component A of an intervention (or of the entire intervention) that are fundamentally distinct from effects caused by component B. The key is to identify exactly what A and B consist of so that it best captures our ordinary attribution of "placebo effects." The proposed theories of placebos we have examined amount to attempts to fill in those placeholders.

A presupposition that most placebo scholars make is that a satisfactory answer to the question of what goes into A and B must ultimately be ontologically meaningful. According to this line of thinking, if the placebo/nonplacebo distinction is to be of any medical importance, it ought to map onto different *kinds* of things. Otherwise, the distinction is just an arbitrary exercise in organizing medicine that is at best pragmatically useful. Like separating laundry into colors and whites, there is no real philosophical lesson to be learned from this ontological exercise other than the limitations of washing machines.

The analyses we have examined rely on the strong intuition that a therapy has two types of components: the characteristic ones and the incidental ones. For a drug, the chemical formulated to treat a certain condition constitutes the characteristic defining component, while the bulking agent, the color and shape of a pill, and the bottle's label are the incidental ones. To be sure, the incidental components are necessary for the function of a drug. After all, a chemical cannot magically enter a human body without some means of delivery. Placebo effects, according to this schema, are effects caused by the incidental components. If this is correct, the task of defining placebo rests on how we distinguish characteristic components from incidental ones.

In 1977, psychiatrist George Engel published an essay "The Need for a New Medical Model: A Challenge for Biomedicine" in the journal *Science* that started a fundamental shift in how we understand medical care. His critical analysis of the biomedical model of disease and treatment led to its gradual demise and the ultimate adoption of a more holistic biopsychosocial model. He explained:

> To provide a basis for understanding the determinants of disease and arriving at rational treatments and patterns of health care, a medical model must also take into account the patient, the social context in which he lives, and the complementary system devised by society to deal with disruptive effects of illness, that is, the physician role and the healthcare system.[67]

The expansion of the "boundaries of treatments" is not limited to clinical care. Public health advocates have convincingly shown that social factors can play incredibly important roles in our health. During a talk a few years ago, the new president of a hospital in the Boston-area highlighted the importance of broadening what we think of as constituting a treatment. A large segment of the hospital's clientele were individuals with a multitude of social challenges. The president recounted that six regular patients in the hospital's emergency department exhausted 50 percent of its annual spending. Delving deeper into their care, she discovered that there were social barriers that made standard treatments inappropriate for them. One particular patient was diabetic and required regular insulin injections. Without access to refrigeration, however, he could not adequately store his stock of insulin, which caused him to miss the vital injections. Although he was always discharged from the hospital with the necessary supply to manage his diabetes, his treatment was not suitable for someone without sustained shelter. The result was that he could not control his blood glucose level and he ended up returning to the emergency room after each acute episode.

The patient's inability to refrigerate his medication, the president saw, was on a par with other clinical challenges (e.g., an allergy to an ingredient in the medication). The hospital began to reconceptualize what makes for good care, and undertook an effort to address some of the social barriers that vulnerable patients face. It started investing in affordable housing and reliable transportation. By focusing too narrowly, clinicians failed to see that adequate treatment constituted more than its physiological components. All elements, regardless of how they are sorted by professional boundaries, can affect a patient's well-being. Ignoring the social determinants of health in the formulation of a treatment is as inappropriate as ignoring contraindications among medications. A narrow physiological understanding of treatment is not only bad metaphysics; it is bad medicine.

The model (e.g., biomedical vs. biopsychosocial model) that we subscribe to not only tells us what a treatment may consist of, it also tells us which part of a treatment is the characteristic and which part the incidental. What recent placebo trials have shown is that there are other factors that can play important roles in the diminishing of pain. The color of the pill, the label that promises pain moderation, the warmth of clinicians and pharmacists, and the cost of the treatment can all contribute to the analgesia. Which of these factors are placebos and which are nonplacebos depends on how we define a therapy and delineate the characteristic from the incidental features.

4.3 Background Theories Distinguish Characteristic and Incidental Features of a Treatment

Jeremy Howick's extension[68] of Adolf Grünbaum's theory[69] of placebo effects convincingly shows how background therapeutic theories delineate the characteristic core of a therapy from its peripheral components. The key to Howick–Grünbaum's approach is the double-relativization of therapies. First, for any given intervention, whether it is a therapy depends on the patient and the disease in question. A sugar pill, argue Howick and Grünbaum, might be a placebo for some individuals. For a diabetic patient, however, it ceases to be a placebo and becomes an active therapy. This nicely captures the intuition behind the idea of relative inertness that we spoke of earlier. Second, Howick and Grünbaum argue that background therapeutic theories tell us which parts of the therapy are characteristic and which parts incidental. Freudian psychoanalysis, for instance, tells us that bringing a patient's repressions to the conscious surface is a characteristic feature of the therapy, while the patient's trust in the therapist and the price point of the fee are merely incidental, even if the latter significantly contribute to the therapy's effectiveness. Meanwhile, cognitive behavioral therapy might consider that repressions are not germane to the therapy; they are at best incidental. So, two different therapeutic theories might look at the same intervention and come to divergent ontologies regarding characteristic and incidental features. Since placebo effects are caused by incidental features, the relativity of therapeutic ontology would mean that whether an effect is placebogenic is also relative to background therapeutic theories.

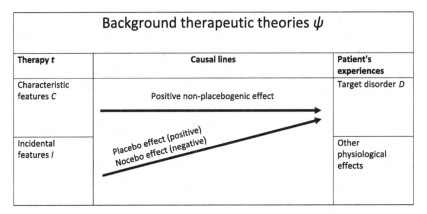

Figure 6 The structure of Howick–Grünbaum's model

For any therapy *t*, it sits within a therapeutic theory ψ that distinguishes the therapy's characteristic features *C* from the incidental ones *I*. Roughly speaking, the therapeutic effects of *t* relative to a particular patient with a specific disease are caused by the characteristic features of *t* that help diminish the disease (see Figure 6). Placebo effects, on the other hand, are caused by the incidental features of *t* that contribute to the elimination of the disease. Nocebo effects are those that exacerbate the condition. By relativizing the concept of *therapy* to individual patients and diseases, Howick and Grünbaum solve the conceptual problem of labeling an active drug a placebo. An active drug like atropine can serve as a placebo so long as it is not causally efficacious with respect to some target disease.

The delineation between the characteristic features of a treatment and the incidental ones, Howick and Grünbaum argue, does not exist in some context-free manner. Rather, the background therapeutic theories of a treatment define the ontology for us. The molecule $C_9H_8O_4$ is the characteristic feature of aspirin not because chemical composition is somehow objectively privileged. The background therapeutic theories of current Western pain management tell us to construe the characteristic features in terms of the chemical makeup of the analgesic and to treat everything else as incidental. The specific/nonspecific problem that has plagued scholars exists because they look for a distinction that is not relative to any background theories. According to Howick and Grünbaum, none is to be found; instead, the line between characteristic and incidental features must be relativized. Of course, we might be wrong about a particular delineation (e.g., a part of a treatment that we thought was not characteristic turns out to be so) but this is not a fatal problem. We constantly modify theories in light of new empirical discoveries and vice versa.

Howick makes four major changes to Grünbaum's initial analysis of placebo to accommodate objections that have been raised against it. For our purposes, I will focus on one of them. John Greenwood argues that Grünbaum's analysis places no limitations on the broader therapeutic theory.[70] Take an entirely artificial theory that says an antibiotic works because the starch contained in the pill kills the bacteria. The doxycycline is just a "bulking agent" and thus incidental. Grünbaum's model would construe the starch as a characteristic factor of the treatment and the doxycycline an incidental factor. Since the drug kills the bacteria, its antibacterial effect would thus be placebogenic. What is nonplacebogenic would be placebogenic according to Grünbaum's view. Furthermore, Grünbaum's analysis fails in the other direction as well: it can incorrectly construe some placebogenic effect as nonplacebogenic. Howick writes:

> Imagine we design a treatment that involves a saline injection and a positive and deceptive suggestion (telling a patient that the injection "involves a powerful drug that is very effective") for treating pain. Imagine further that we classify the saline as incidental and the positive suggestion as characteristic. Background knowledge tells us that the "characteristic" feature of such a treatment is likely to be effective, leading one who adheres strictly to Grünbaum's scheme to classify the treatment as a non-placebo. This seems absurd.[71]

To avoid these "absurd" results, Howick suggests that we place two additional constraints on what counts as an acceptable background therapeutic theory. For any characteristic feature of a therapy:

(1) It is not the patient's expectancy that causes a treatment to be effective, and
(2) It has an incremental benefit on the target disorder over a legitimate placebo control in a well-controlled trial.

Condition (1) blocks the counterexample that Howick outlines since the effectiveness of the therapy in that example comes entirely from the patient's expectancy. Condition (2) circumvents Greenwood's objection by ruling out background therapeutic theories that are not supported by well-controlled placebo trials. Presumably, the wacky theories in Greenwood's example enjoy no empirical support.

A worry with Howick's solution is that there might very well be other means to elicit placebo effects and his condition (1) will have to be amended with every new discovery. Consider the BBM$^+$. Suppose a patient's perception of their pain diminishes because of a Bayesian revision. This kind of analgesia is placebogenic. We can then construct a deviant background therapeutic theory that considers the Bayesian revision a characteristic feature. The placebo effect in this example would thus be considered nonplacebogenic. Howick can certainly add another restriction to accommodate this counterexample but there is a deeper worry behind this ad hoc strategy. The main goal of Howick's restrictions is to ensure that the model captures our commonsense judgments of which effects are placebogenic and which not. But since background therapeutic theories draw a line between characteristic and incidental features, by building into the definition of *characteristic feature* that it must not cause placebo effects (e.g., effects via expectancy), Howick risks a circular analysis. His approach would essentially amount to the claim that C is a characteristic feature (as determined by background therapeutic theory ψ) only if C does not cause placebo effects. Since placebos lie among the incidental feature of a therapy, we arrive at the (almost) trivial analysis that C is not a placebo only if C does not cause placebo effects.

Rather than seeing the objections raised against Grünbaum's model as threats to the overall approach, I argue that they contain some valuable insights about the nature of placebo. Consider a future in which the elicitation of placebo effects is as reliable and consistent as typical medical treatments. In this world, we have robust background therapeutic theories that support the use of placebos as treatments. For example, we know that OLPs can significantly lessen the symptoms of IBS. We might even know exactly how the swallowing of these pills changes the neurophysiology of IBS patients to bring about improvement.

As clinicians learn more about the nature of placebo effects, therapeutic placebos will likely be incorporated into conventional medicine and this can lead to an odd result. Since the distinction between characteristic features and incidental features is determined by the background therapeutic theories, as therapeutic placebos become absorbed by theories of conventional medicine, the cause of placebogenic therapeutic effects will migrate to the domain of characteristic features. And, if placebos are incidental features that cause positive changes in a patient's health outcomes, then placebo therapies will no longer be caused by the incidental features; hence, they would paradoxically cease to be placebogenic. One possible solution is that we will need to change the name OLP to avoid the awkwardness of placebo treatments without placebos. Perhaps we could call OLP pills "activation pills." Again, this would not be a defect of our analysis. The possibility of incorporating therapeutic placebos into conventional medicine and thus erasing its outsider status is merely a variant of Phil Fontanarosa and George Lundberg's *Journal of American Medical Association* (*JAMA*) editorial that there is no alternative medicine, only medicine well-supported by evidence.[72] As placebo therapies gain effectiveness, they are absorbed into standard medical theories. This, in turn, revises the line between characteristic and incidental features such that what was once considered placebo effects caused by incidental features are now therapeutic effects caused by characteristic features. Grünbaum's depiction perfectly accommodates the interaction between a treatment's status (placebo or not) and the background medical theories. The division between placebo and non-placebo effects is as fluid as the line between characteristic and incidental features of a treatment.

There is nothing fundamentally different about placebo therapies. Howick's perceived need to supplement Grünbaum's model is partly rooted in his assumption that the placebo/nonplacebo distinction is ontologically significant in the sense that it exists independently of any relativization. The fact that a deviant therapeutic theory might reconstrue a placebo effect as nonplacebogenic is threatening only because we are wedded to this realist impulse. The flexibility of Grünbaum's model to alter the placebo status of an intervention (in light of changing background theories) is a virtue of the model, not a vice.

The idea that broader theories supply the semantics or conceptual framework of a (scientific) practice is nothing new. Thomas Kuhn has certainly advocated for a version of meaning holism that relativizes the meaning of theoretical terms to their paradigms. Similarly, W. V. O. Quine and Ludwig Wittgenstein have both claimed that the meaning of a term depends on the language in which it resides. It is, indeed, expected that the background therapeutic theories would supply the concepts, ontology, and metaphysics of medicine. Semantic holism implies that wacky background therapeutic theories would give us wacky ontologies. The key is not to place a priori constraints on theories but to examine our process of theory selection when a wacky theory gets through. As the cliché goes, "If you don't want stupid prizes, don't play stupid games."

4.4 The Messiness of Background Theories Makes Defining Placebo Messy

Therapeutic theories of modern medicine are often filled with arbitrary and internally incoherent conceptual distinctions. The frequency of symptom experiences, for example, is a common criterion in diagnosing a pathology. The 5th edition of the *Diagnostic and Statistical Manual of Mental Disorders* (DSM-5) introduced persistent complex bereavement disorder – a new diagnosis (albeit, controversial) for individuals who struggle with the death of a loved one, which, according to DSM-5, is experienced by 2.4–4.8 percent of individuals.[73] First among the diagnostic criteria, an individual who is suffering from pathological grieving must direct the grief toward the death of someone with whom the individual had a close relationship. Another criterion requires that, for an adult, persistent yearning for the deceased lasts at least twelve months.

Like much of DSM-5, a strict application of diagnostic criteria would miss a great deal of the nuances of the human psyche. These coarse-grained criteria can serve as useful guidelines for clinicians. But there is surely nothing special about the twelve-month mark such that someone goes from normal to pathological grieving overnight. And just as they may grieve over the death of a loved one, they can grieve over the death of a political leader or a family pet (although they might not form the same sort of close interpersonal relationships). From nosology to etiology, modern medicine is a theoretical behemoth that is not just informed by methodological and theoretical tenets, but is also the result of historical legacies, turf wars, financial incentives, clinical applicability, fads, and social and personal peculiarities. Unsurprisingly, medicine is like other human institutions with structures that are messy, arbitrary, and incoherent at times.

More than merely providing the micro-ontology of treatments (e.g., what part of a treatment is characteristic and what part is incidental) from the top down, background therapeutic theories are also affected by innovations in medical technology from the bottom up. In his detailed survey of the history of theories of depression since the 1950s, Shai Mulinari argues that the emergence of new laboratory techniques that helped discover new neurotransmitters in the late 1970s and early 1980s opened up the possibility of novel psychotropics that can modify these neurotransmitters.[74] With the advent of selective serotonin reuptake inhibitors (SSRIs) and the tremendous resources pharmaceutical companies spent on them, the new receptor theory of depression gained prominence even though empirical evidence was lacking at the time. To put it plainly, new ways of detecting neurobiological activities and new means of moderating them propelled the receptor theory of depression that could take advantage of these pharmacological products. Rather than first identifying a plausible theory of depression and then developing adequate responses to the pathology, new drugs drove the development of theories of depression that could take advantage of the former as possible treatments. The history of depression is a history of drugs looking for a theory. This upward revision spurred on by "extrascientific" pressure makes it even less likely that background therapeutic theories have got the ontology of disease and treatment "right." The dominance of a therapeutic theory is often due to pragmatic or extrascientific reasons.

Background therapeutic theories can contain internal incoherence which renders the ontology of treatments fundamentally unstable. Consider a holistic approach to transitioning from one sex to another. Sociologist Stefan Hirschauer explains that the multidisciplinary approach to transitioning contains three different methods of determining sex.[75] A psychologist takes sexual identification as primarily patient-driven; that is, the patient self-identifies as a member of a sex and the psychologist confirms it by noting the patient's sustained commitment to living as a member of that sex. Once the patient has been psychologically cleared to undergo hormone treatments, an endocrinologist determines the starting sex and ending sex via measurements of testosterone and estrogen levels. Finally, a surgeon physically sculpts the patient's body so that it presents the appropriate anatomy. All three domains have divergent standards for determining membership of a sex, and how the different components of the treatment are reconciled is a matter of extramedical deliberation. For instance, power dynamics among the clinicians might lead the endocrinologist to follow the recommendation of the therapist even if hormonal levels do not agree with the former's diagnosis.

Among the features of holistic sex reassignment therapy, which features are characteristic and which incidental? Is the holistic therapy mainly about psychology such that the hormonal treatments and the surgical alterations are incidental, only serving to ensure a smoother transition? Or perhaps it is the surgical component that is the active feature while the other two are merely supportive? It should be clear that we cannot arrive at an answer without considering pragmatic factors such as patients' preferences and the legal and political ramifications.

Often, there is nothing within background therapeutic theories which tells us exactly how to draw a line between characteristic and incidental features. To settle the matter, we must appeal to extramedical and pragmatic considerations. Background theories in medicine underdetermine how we ought to adjudicate disagreements about the ontology of therapies. If we look to define *placebo effects* as those that arise out of the incidental features of a treatment, and if the delineation of incidental features of a treatment depends on background therapeutic theories that are messy and arbitrary at times, it is not surprising that definitions of placebo inherit the same messiness and arbitrariness. The difficulties in coming up with an acceptable definition of *placebo* partly come from our failure to appreciate the messiness of medical theories.

There is a second and related reason that helps explain why defining placebo has been so difficult, and it concerns the context-dependency of identifying a salient cause. One of the distinguishing characteristics of medicine is the belief that our universe is guided by causality (at least for familiar medium-sized objects: those larger than molecules and smaller than celestial bodies). Clinicians might not know exactly what underlying mechanism brings about the effects of a treatment but, by and large, they believe that the therapeutic process is a causal physical one. The hope is that we will eventually uncover, in finer causal detail, the precise mechanisms that connect a treatment to its clinical outcomes. For modern medicine, the metaphysical commonality that ties clinicians and researchers (and perhaps some patients) together is the belief that physical causality is responsible for all therapeutic processes – or what I refer to as folk causality.

The nature of causality has puzzled philosophers for centuries. The identification of salient causes (*the* cause) is often a matter of pragmatics. What caused World War I? Contributing factors range from the rise of nationalism to the competition for colonies and their raw materials. Which of these factors count as *the* cause depends on the context of the discourse. A military historian might focus on strategic considerations such as the tight schedule of mobilization as the main contributor to the causal chain of events. A Marxist critic, on the other hand, might focus on the emergence of organized labor that caused nation states to initiate armed conflicts to blunt the growing power of workers. It makes little sense to speak of a context-independent salient cause.

Any treatment contains numerous components that contribute to the improvement of a patient. An antibiotic improves their well-being regarding an infection, but it cannot function effectively without the incidental components including the bulking material, competent care providers, and a system to make the medication affordable and accessible. Is any one of these factors more indispensable than another? The pragmatic context of the discourse guides our causal focus. The traditional identification of active ingredients with the pharmacological substance in a drug is useful for many practical reasons. For example, in standardizing care, it is far easier to talk about identical care if we delineate care in terms of pharmacological metrics. Even if the warmth of a clinician does contribute to the effectiveness of a drug, it is far harder to quantify and dispense equally warm care. Structural demands such as our commitment to equity, insurance companies' reimbursement and coverage schedules, and the financial incentives involved in drug development all give us reasons to focus on the pharmacological substance as *the* characteristic feature of a treatment. Of course, we can modify or abandon some of these structures that surround the practice of medicine, but the key here is to understand that micro-ontology depends on broader pragmatic factors.

As much as Howick and Grünbaum are on the correct path when they point out that background therapeutic theories demarcate characteristics factors from the incidental ones, they have not gone far enough. The context-dependency of causal saliency and the pragmatic factors of a discourse determine how we slice up our therapeutic ontology. The main reason why defining *placebo* has been so challenging is that the task implicitly demands a context-independent way to specify the characteristic features of a treatment. The fact remains, however, that how we slice up the ontology of a treatment is entirely dependent on pragmatic factors and so long as we look for context-independent distinctions we will continue to fall short in our quest to define *placebo*.

As a positive thesis, I will propose a rough definition of *placebo* and *placebo effect* by building upon the work of Howick and Grünbaum. The micro-ontology of a therapy is determined by background therapeutic theories that can be internally incoherent, filled with gaps, or adopted for pragmatic reasons. A placebo effect consists of

(1) a positive (or at least nonnegative) effect a patient experiences relative to a disease state that is caused by some incidental feature; and

(2) mechanisms underlying the placebo effect that remain relatively unknown.

As we gain more precise knowledge of the causal mechanisms (and can elicit placebo effects more consistently), we are less likely to consider them placebogenic. This last feature captures some of the intuitions we have about placebo effects. If we understand the precise mechanisms that track how the ingestion of a pill can alleviate the symptoms of IBS, its therapeutic benefits shift from placebogenic to nonplacebogenic. Finally, these two conditions adhere to what legal scholars refer to as the inverse ratio rule. For instance, with regard to entrapment, a defendant needs to show that (1) they were induced to commit the crime and (2) they were not predisposed to criminal activities. However, as more evidence is provided for one of the conditions, the need to satisfy the other condition decreases. The same can be said for my proposed two conditions for placebo. As we learn more about the causal pathway of a placebo effect, whether it stems from incidental features of a treatment becomes less important. The reason is obvious: the growth of causal knowledge will likely lead to revision of our background medical theories so that they would incorporate the causes of placebo effects into the characteristic features of the treatment. The knowledge of placebo effects, in this sense, affects background medical theories, which in turn helps redraw the line between characteristic and incidental features of treatments.[76] This dynamic – a feedback loop – between research and theory is what makes defining a static notion of *placebo* impossible.

4.5 Placebos and Authenticity

This section ends by looking at an underappreciated ethical problem with placebo therapies. The Taiwanese American author Charles Yu published a short story "The Future of Work: Placebo" in *Wired* magazine that nicely captures some of the moral unease with placebo therapies.[77] In Yu's future, clinicians caring for dying patients are no longer medical professionals in our sense. Instead of clinicians trained in medicine, actors portray them and a fantastic artificial intelligence (AI) supplies the prompts through a tablet telling the actors what to say and do. Actors continue to look and act the part; after all, there are placebogenic benefits of an empathetic provider, trained to place a warm hand at the right time in the right way. Depending on the level of service paid for (e.g., Basic Plus or Premium), the actors will provide different degrees of placebogenic care. A witty joke that would liven up a moment, for instance, is only available to those who paid extra.

A patient, Jenny, is dying from stage IV carcinoma. At the level of service she has purchased, the most Brad – an actor who plays the clinician – can do is to console her with a comforting hand. Disclosing her poor prognosis is beyond his competency, the tablet tells him. The frustration of not being able to offer basic human compassion and behave authentically, not as a fake doctor but as another human being in the presence of a dying person, makes it difficult for him to stay in character. Soon enough, Jenny becomes wise to the charade and asks Brad to tell her more about his real life. He confesses that he had wanted to be a fake heart surgeon but failed the audition. As Brad, prompted by the tablet, asks for permission to place his hand on her, Jenny slowly drifts away.

The brilliance of Yu's story lies in his ability to capture the incongruity between the placebo performatives and the authenticity so critical for care, medicine, and empathy. If an AI can perfect the diagnostic task, what is there left for most clinicians to do but be an effective deliverer of the placebo effects? In the case of a dying patient, there is no more to be done therapeutically; the only thing that remains is the experience. Incidental features of care, so to speak, become the only features.

What is most disturbing about the story is that the practice of actor-care runs contrary to some of the most cherished values in medicine. When I am dying, I do not just want someone to make my transition comfortable. I want someone to care about my death. I want to share the dying experience: the inevitable and at times grateful end that is nevertheless saddening for the dying. If it turns out to be the case that a clinician's demeanor contributes to my dying experience, I still wish that my care providers place their hands on me, not because it improves my experience but because they care.

What goes for end-stage care in Yu's story goes for clinical care in general. As we learn more about the therapeutic benefits of the "performatives," a tension arises between caring for caring's sake and caring for therapeutic's sake. It might certainly be the case that many of us would trade the former for the latter, but placebo therapies open the possibility of kindness, compassion, and warmth for therapy's sake. Being kind to someone because it is good for them seems to undermine a crucial aspect of humanism; that is, our solidarity in living a life so often filled with tragedies.

Ethical issues in placebo usage have largely focused on the problem of deceptive treatments and the use of placebo control in clinical trials. Yu's story identifies an unexpected incongruity between placebo therapies and authenticity. Just as our attempt to provide an adequate definition of *placebo* has led to a reconsideration of the boundaries of treatment, I am certain that the use of therapeutic placebos will uncover ethical issues that will require us to reflect on the goals of medicine and the nature of care.

What is remarkable about placebos lies not merely in their surprising physiological effects. Rather, they force us to reexamine what constitutes a treatment, expand the arbitrary limits of medical care (as advocates of social determinants of health have done), and ask ourselves what we really want out of medicine – and out of life. In the last section, I will outline some immediate problems that philosophers and placebo researchers ought to tackle in the study of placebos.

5 The Near Future of Placebo Research

5.1 Methodological Problems

In a controlled trial, an ideal control ought to be as similar to the experimental treatment as possible except for the characteristic features whose therapeutic efficacy is being studied. The use of active placebos – interventions that have salient effects – is entirely appropriate so long as the effects do not undermine the internal validity of the trial (i.e., unbiased data properly support the hypothesis).

The problem of unblinding (i.e., discovering to which arm a subject has been assigned), however, does not concern subjects' ability to guess correctly their "arm identity" (i.e., whether they are in the active or control arm). If one's *belief* in the therapeutic efficacy of an intervention affects its actual efficacy, the veracity of one's guess is of secondary importance. As long as *beliefs* or *expectations* affect the intervention's effectiveness, the clinical results can be tainted by placebo effects. The use of controls to minimize placebo effects should therefore aim to equalize subjects' *perceived* ability to discern their arm identity across the experimental arms.

In randomizing the assignment of subjects to experimental arms, the goal is to secure in all subjects a similar degree of confidence in terms of their arm identity. A trial that has two experimental arms randomly assigns half the subjects to each arm to cultivate in them a 50 percent certainty in their arm identity. Of course, this is just one way to equalize subjects' confidence in their arm identity. Imagine that researchers managed to ensure that all subjects have a 75 percent confidence level toward their arm identity. The fact that subjects' confidence level deviates from 50 percent confidence does not affect the internal validity of the trial. Since, according to the additive model, the efficacy of an experimental treatment is the difference between the active arm and the control arm, if outcomes in both arms contain the same amount of placebo effects, the net difference would remain the same. Randomization is a convenient way to equalize subjects' confidence with regard to their arm identity, but there is no reason in principle that all subjects ought to have a 50 percent confidence level.

For the purpose of external validity (i.e., how well a study's results can be generalized to the public at large), equalizing subjects' confidence with regard to arm identity is not sufficient. In selecting a cohort for a clinical trial, researchers aim to match subjects as closely as possible to the demographic of individuals who will eventually use the treatment. Selecting only college males enrolled in Introduction to Psychology as the subjects would obviously raise some red flags for any global generalizations.

The fact that typical randomized controlled trials involve subjects that are not certain whether they receive treatments should make us wonder whether they are representational of the end-users in the real world. After all, when I take a drug, I assign a much higher confidence level that I am taking the intended drug than 50 percent. How much should we worry about this incongruity from the point of view of placebo effects? With a higher confidence level, an end-user in the real world might experience a greater amount of placebo effect. The total effectiveness of the treatment would thus be greater than the results from a clinical trial. However, the relative benefit of the treatment – *verum* effect divided by total effect – would diminish as a result. Since the total effectiveness of the treatment for the general public is larger (because of the additional placebo effect), the percentage of *verum* effect brought on by the treatment would thus be smaller. In other words, in the wild, we should expect the relative effectiveness of a treatment to be smaller than what is demonstrated in the respective randomized placebo-controlled trials. One way to avoid this result is to bring the confidence level of subjects with regard to their arm identity on a par with end-users' confidence. This will, of course, introduce a host of ethical challenges; for example, misinforming subjects in both the active and control arms that 90 percent of them would receive the experimental treatment.

There is another methodological assumption made in controlled trials that is underexplored. In posttrial surveys that look to determine if unblinding has taken place, subjects' confidence levels are often pooled together in statistical modeling. Pooling confidence levels of subjects in the active and control arms together is obviously problematic. Suppose 100 percent of the subjects in the active arm believed they did not receive the treatment and 100 percent of those in the control arm believed that they did. A pooling of those values might give researchers the mistaken impression that 50 percent of the subjects thought they received the treatment; thus, the trial managed to maintain universal confidence level.

Pooling subjects within each experimental arm might also generate misleading results. The practice assumes that a placebo effect is proportional to the confidence level of the subject about receiving the treatment. Consider a placebo arm with ten subjects. Suppose three of the subjects were 75 percent confident that they were in the active arm, three were 25 percent confident, and four 50 percent confident. Pooling their confidence levels together would give us an average confidence level of 50 percent. This result accurately reflects the magnitude of the placebo effect in the control arm only if we assume a linear relationship between confidence level and placebo effect. Suppose placebo effects "kick in" at around 40 percent confidence level and diminish after 70 percent. The amount of placebo effect would be significantly smaller than if there were a linear relationship. Moreover, pooled averages might incorrectly tell us that two arms in a study had the same confidence level; thus, placebo effects were properly controlled. If subjects had radically different distributions of confidence levels in the two arms, the pooled average might mislead us into concluding that blinding was properly maintained.[78]

Another concern with regard to placebo-controlled trials is the common assumption that the additive model is unproblematic. Recall that according to this model, the therapeutic benefit of an intervention is the difference between the outcomes of the active arm and the control arm. The model assumes that there are no interactions between the experimental treatment and the baseline placebo effects. For a given intervention t that is being tested in the active arm, it consists of C (the characteristic features that are missing in the placebo control) and I (the incidental features that are perfectly replicated by an ideal control). The standard assumption is that C and I do not interact within t. Nonetheless, if the characteristic features C of t affect the placebogenic magnitude of I, then the controlled trial would incorrectly estimate the therapeutic effectiveness of t. Given the potential impact this assumption has on trial results and the ubiquitous reliance on the additive model, it is unfortunate that only a few scholars such as Katja Boehm et al. and Charles Weijer have raised concerns with the additive model.[79]

An example can better illustrate the worry. Consider a novel analgesic pill being tested against a placebo-controlled equivalent. If the BBM$^+$ is correct, placebogenic analgesia might be the result of subjects' turning down the pain signal when prompted with cues such as the caring demeanor of the clinicians. Suppose that the novel analgesic pill being tested makes it more difficult for subjects to detect clinicians' demeanor; for example, clinicians come across as

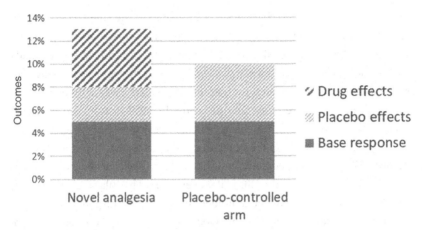

Figure 7 An example of interactions between a treatment and its placebo effects

more robotic and uncaring to the subjects. The result is a decrease of placebo-genic analgesia in the active arm. Since the additive model defines the therapeutic effectiveness of a treatment as the difference in outcomes between the active and the control arms, the trial would underestimate the effectiveness of the novel analgesia (see Figure 7).

The additive model only looks at the net outcome of each arm and compare them to determine the effectiveness of the experimental treatment. There is no mechanism to check whether the experimental treatment affects the baseline placebo effects. This example illustrates the possibility that the additive model would give us the wrong estimate of a treatment's effectiveness if it affects subjects' placebo responses.

It might be suggested that it matters little whether the pill's analgesic power comes from its characteristic features or from the incidental features; ultimately, patients experience less pain. However, from an epistemic point of view, a trial in which the experimental treatment affects placebo effects gives us the wrong measurement of the therapeutic effectiveness of the treatment. The entire point of a placebo-controlled trial is to determine the true benefit of a treatment. Ignoring the problem here, at the very least, runs contrary to the purpose of placebo-controlled trials. In addition, the hypothetical scenario here is akin to any interaction between, for instance, an experimental drug and its bulking agent. In the example above, the novel analgesia works less efficiently than it should because it negatively affects the placebogenic power of the drug. If we can remove the features that undercut the baseline placebo effects, the treatment would thus be more effective. The only way this can be done reliably is to have a better understanding of placebo effects and identify the ways they can be modified.

While the scenario described poses a problem for the internal validity of placebo-controlled trials, there are potential worries that impact the trials' external validity. Consider the concept of *placebo responders* – individuals who are more likely to experience placebo effects or to experience them with greater magnitudes. The search for placebo responders essentially began with the advent of modern research into placebos. In 1954, a team led by Louis Lasagna examined whether placebo responders were more likely to have certain personality dispositions.[80] One of their observations was that "[i]n answer to the question 'What sort of people do you like best?' [placebo responders] were more likely to respond with 'Oh, I like everyone.' The [placebo responders] were more frequently active church-goers than the non-[responders] and had less formal education."[81] Easy-going, God-fearing, and less educated folks are apparently more responsive to placebos. More recently, a trial suggested that pessimists were more likely to experience placebogenic symptoms than optimists when told that they had ingested an active medication.[82]

A clinical trial that contains an unusually high number of placebo responders would understate the relative effectiveness of a treatment since the proportion of *verum* response to placebo response would be smaller given the greater placebo response. Consider trial A that has a higher proportion of subjects who are placebo responders than trial B (see Figure 8).

The additive model tells us that in trial A, the effectiveness of the intervention is 2.5 (represented by the verum bar). The therapeutic difference is the same in trial B. However, because of the higher concentration of placebo responders in trial A (distributed randomly and equally across the two arms), there is a greater placebo response in both arms of trial A. The relative effectiveness of the experimental intervention is the ratio of its effectiveness over the control response. For trial A, it is 2.5 divided by 8 which is 31 percent; that is, the

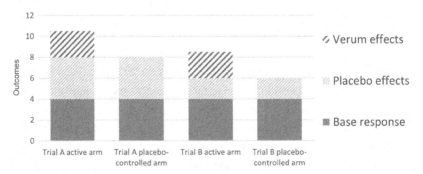

Figure 8 High percentage of placebo responders (trial A) versus normal percentage of placebo responders (trial B)

experimental intervention is 31 percent more effective than the control. Although the therapeutic effectiveness of the experimental intervention in trial B is also 2.5, the fact that the control response is 6 means that the relative effectiveness of the treatment is 42 percent. By having a higher concentration of placebo responders in trial A, even though the subjects are randomly and evenly assigned across the two arms, trial A underestimates the relative effectiveness of the experimental intervention.

It is here that knowledge of the underlying mechanisms for placebo effects can help ensure better external validity. Suppose the BBM^+, that placebo responses result from belief revisions, is correct. In order to predict the magnitude of a subject's placebogenic reaction, we would need to know not only the Bayesian algorithm the brain uses to revise beliefs, we would also need to know the relevant beliefs and their probability values for the subject. In predicting how a person reacts to a placebo, we need to find out what they believe in. With the decline of reductionism in philosophy, the future of placebo research and clinical medicine might require that we likewise move away from trying to reduce human conditions to biophysiological phenomena. Focusing on the level of beliefs and not their neurological underpinnings might be of far greater usefulness in understanding placebo effects. To do otherwise would be as hopeless as trying to predict your opponent's chess moves by looking at their individual neurons and genes.

5.2 Developing and Approving Placebo Treatments

Guidelines on clinical trials from regulatory agencies like the US Food and Drug Administration (FDA) do not straightforwardly apply to research on placebo therapies. For instance, before initiating a Phase I clinical trial, researchers generally must provide preclinical evidence. This is particularly important for "first-in-human" trials to ensure that human subjects are not unduly harmed in the exploration of new treatments. Preclinical evidence for a pharmaceutical trial, for instance, usually includes data from animal models and what researchers know about effective means of delivery.

These issues are clearly more complicated in the case of placebo research. With the exception of a very few published trials, there has been little research on placebo effects among nonhuman animals. As we saw earlier, it is an open question as to whether and how much cognition is necessary for placebogenic reactions. If it turns out to be the case that some cognitive capacities are necessary for a being to have a placebogenic reaction, then it would be impossible for any organisms that lack those capacities to experience placebo effects. As a result, preclinical evidence from typical animal models might be impossible if they lack sufficiently robust cognition.

Having a clear idea of the proper means of delivery can also pose a problem for placebo effects. Numerous trials have suggested that the manner of delivery can affect the magnitude of placebo effects (e.g., injections generate greater placebo effects than swallowing pills). In other words, how a placebo is delivered is itself part of the placebo. Without experimenting on the placebos and learning more about the impact delivery has on placebo effects, it would be extraordinarily difficult to say anything concrete about the proper means of delivery prior to a typical Phase I trial.

With the emergence of OLP research, the seemingly unavoidable fact needs to be considered that the lack of double-blinding entails that evidence from these trials will be of lower epistemic quality. The problem is that subjects and experimenters can easily determine subjects' arm identity: open-label means that subjects are explicitly told that they are receiving placebos. Since unblinding can lead to biases (e.g., subjects' desire to please experimenters or experimenters' desire for a successful experiment), evidence from these trials would seem to be necessarily inferior, all things being equal. One might, for instance, make sure that outcome evaluators are not told which arm the subjects belong to. But this mechanism would only keep clinicians blinded; it would not help with subjects' awareness of their arm identity. To be sure, the singular fixation on double-blinded placebo-controlled randomized clinical trials as the gold standard of evidence-based medicine is likely inappropriate. Other sources of evidence can surpass the quality of data from randomized clinical trials.[83] Nonetheless, OLP trials would need to compensate for the loss of evidential quality by, say, increasing sample size. Coupled with the generally small cohorts of published clinical trials on placebo effects, increasing sample size would be of paramount importance for the immediate future of placebo research.

Finally, the structure of knowledge production in medicine works against placebo research. The pharmaceutical industry's willingness to invest significantly in treatment development is rooted in its expectation that a successful treatment can bring about a financial windfall, more than enough to compensate for its research investment and the expense of other failed projects. Therapeutic use of placebos, however, is not likely to generate the same level of financial return. As a result, there is little incentive for pharmaceutical companies to invest in placebo research. Moreover, the potential financial reward of launching a successful new drug provides a perverse incentive to medicalize human conditions that can only be managed with pharmacological interventions. If a company can convince the public that a human condition (e.g., an elevated level of cholesterol that falls below some pathological threshold) is really a medical condition that needs to be treated (e.g., prediabetes), they can easily market a drug that can moderate the condition by medicalizing it. One of the basic tenets of placebo therapies is that, in many cases, our physiology already contains the mechanisms necessary to improve our health and to recover from ailments. In this sense, placebo therapies fly in the face of the dominant culture of specialized and external medicine; that is, to feel better, a patient must seek the help of medical experts who provide treatments that our innate physiology is incapable of supplying. Not only does this undermine the financial picture of present healthcare, it also threatens the monopoly of skills and knowledge modern medicine possesses. For those who have much to lose, there is every reason not to support placebo research.

As we learn more about the power of placebos, it becomes ever more tempting to ask how much conventional medical interventions outperform their placebo counterparts. A senior and well-respected clinician once said to me, "We all know that about a third of all current treatments are either useless or harmful; the hard part is figuring out which third." Research comparing accepted treatments to placebos has occasionally led to the decline of the treatments when they do not outperform placebos. One of the most noteworthy examples is the vertebroplasty trial by Kallmes' team. A study by Fabrice Smieliauskas, Sandi Lam, and David Howard shows that the number of vertebroplasties performed in a Florida hospital after the publication of the negative reviews decreased by 51.5 percent.[84] However, when Jeremy Howick et al.'s 2013 analysis of 152 published clinical studies of some standard treatments found little statistical differences between the interventions and placebo controls, the study barely made any impact on clinical practice.[85] To be sure, there are good reasons to ensure that changes in clinical practice come about slowly; we do not want standard treatments to change direction like a weather vane. Nonetheless, we ought to keep in mind that therapeutic changes are disruptive and that no one wants change unless it is necessary. Placebo research that highlights the effect of placebos at the expense of conventional therapies will likely be met with some skeptical resistance. In order to ensure healthy support for placebo research, it behooves us to be mindful of these biases.

5.3 Incorporating Placebos into Clinical Care

The use of placebos continues to carry a stigma. Placebo interventions are still referred to as "dummy pills" and the equivalent of "getting nothing." Those who respond to placebo interventions are "gullible," "foolish," and "uneducated." In a debriefing after a recent experiment with which I am familiar, subjects who responded positively during the trial grew angry when they were told they were in the placebo arm. The debriefing team felt so unsafe that they asked if the remaining interviews could be carried out over the phone or via email.

Outside the context of placebos, however, the idea that beliefs and rituals can have dramatic physiological impacts is hardly controversial. A study conducted by Shanshan Li's team published in *JAMA Internal Medicine* concluded that "[f]requent attendance at religious services was associated with significantly lower risk of all-cause, cardiovascular, and cancer mortality among women."[86] The conclusion that attending religious services might lower one's risk of dying was not met with dismissal or ridicule. Similarly, on the topic of stress management, we are often told that positive thinking and optimism can increase life span, help prevent depression, improve resistance to illness, and reduce the risk of death from cancer. The idea that aligning one's attitudes and beliefs can provide health benefits has become an important pillar in the popular conception of self-care and mind and body medicine. Yet, the very possibility that the ritual of swallowing a pill (really, taking steps to heal) can be an effective therapy in and of itself is met with disbelief and those who fall for it regarded as simpletons. It is placebos' unwarranted stigma that contributes to the resistance to incorporate them into allopathic medicine. To change this, it is imperative that we learn from experts in health communication to find the most effective way to combat stigmas.

As placebos and placebo therapies become normalized, there will be a need to find ways to incorporate them into the toolkit of treatments. Focusing on pharmaceuticals, the logistical and bureaucratic chain that currently guides access to drugs, means there will be little to say regarding placebos. Health insurance providers do not generally cover placebos. Even in the case of clinical trials, the cost of placebo controls is typically shouldered by the research teams. Adding placebos to insurance providers' formularies (i.e., the list of drugs covered by a healthcare plan) will not be a simple matter of inputting a new drug. The causes that give rise to placebo effects go far beyond a simple pill. Frequent contacts with caring clinicians, retail pharmacists who are properly trained to provide the necessary support, and the label and pricing of the pill can all be integral to a treatment's success.

In traditional treatments, the line between the characteristic and incidental features of a treatment is fairly clearly drawn. Health insurance providers will cover the cost of a drug, say, but not the cost of transportation to bring patients to their pharmacies even though, without the latter, the former sits unused. Given the ritualistic or performative nature of placebo therapies, the line between the characteristic and incidental features becomes much more blurred. To fold placebo treatments into conventional care, some of these hard philosophical issues, such as the micro-ontology of treatments, needs to be rethought.

Placebo therapies also present some unique practical problems. As some studies have suggested, the price point of a treatment can affect its causal efficacy. Placebo pharmaceuticals might be significantly cheaper to manufacture. Suppose regulations exist limiting how much a pharmaceutical manufacturer can charge for a drug relative to the cost of manufacturing it. Should pricing be kept artificially high in order to sustain a placebo treatment's efficacy? This is more than merely a hypothetical scenario. Conflicts between placebo effects and well-intended regulatory policies already exist.[87] Consider the Federal Court's judgment in Australia in 2015 that Nurofen misled consumers with the labeling of its ibuprofens. Although Nurofen sold its painkillers with different packaging and labeling (e.g., for migraine pain, period pain, back pain, etc.), they were all in fact the same drug with the same dosage.[88] The court's ruling led to the removal of the products and the prohibition of the diverse labeling practice. As important as it is to ensure consumers are not misled, there might be a therapeutic cost associated with the prohibition of "misleading labeling." Given what we know of placebo effects, a drug that is specifically marketed to treat migraine pain might indeed perform better than one that says otherwise. By making the labeling more transparent, the court might have unintentionally made patients worse off by denying them an effective treatment. Indeed, what should we say about a misleading practice that brings about the effects that it lies about? An energy drink promises enhanced cognitive performance which does not exist as determined by placebo-controlled trials. Yet, by lying about its enhancive power, the drink actually delivers the enhancive power. Is the promise of enhanced cognitive performance false advertising?

Returning again to vertebroplasty, imagine that in light of the failure of vertebroplasty to outperform the sham version, insurance providers stop reimbursing for the practice and professional organizations remove it from their list of approved procedures. This seems to be a paradigmatic example of clinical medicine responding quickly to new evidence – something that most of us would laud. But, the removal of vertebroplasty as a treatment option does not mean that it will be replaced by the sham treatment. Recall that vertebroplasty (and its sham equivalent) is remarkably effective when compared to no treatment. Removing vertebroplasty without any alternatives leaves patients with no effective treatment for compressed back fractures. A simple rule that we should only provide procedures that outperform placebo controls might paradoxically rob patients of effective treatments.

The role of beliefs in placebo effects generates some fascinating questions about medical education. The series of acupuncture trials conducted by German researchers strongly suggests that the therapeutic benefits of acupuncture are placebogenic. Neither the location of the needle's placement nor the penetration of a subject's skin appears to be necessary to induce the benefits. Many academic institutions offer degrees and certificates in acupuncture and state licensing boards require substantial educational training along with supervised clinical experience.

As an example, Massachusetts requires almost 2,000 hours of clinical and didactic training before a person is permitted to perform acupuncture. How are we to reconcile the placebogenic benefits of acupuncture with the robust educational requirements? Perhaps the practitioners' belief in the therapeutic power of acupuncture (as a *verum*) is necessary. If so, then going through the rigorous training and becoming a "true believer" is critical for an acupuncturist to deliver effective therapies, even if the faithful following of their training adds little to the treatment's effectiveness. How extensive should this facade be? Should institutions that offer training be true believers as well? Should acupuncture clinics be filled with evidence of the legitimacy of acupuncture (e.g., charts identifying meridian points, certificates and diplomas testifying to extensive training, and artifacts that communicate cultural alignments conducive to effective treatments)? On the other hand, if it turns out to be the case that placebo effects do not require beliefs (i.e., they can be elicited via some autonomic system), then so long as clinicians know how to initiate them, their understanding of the treatment theories becomes secondary. If so, why bother enacting robust educational requirements, let alone charge expensive fees for the training? This problem does not just occur with acupuncture. Any treatments whose therapeutic benefits are largely placebogenic have to confront the same issue. If arthroscopic knee surgeries are essentially placebo treatments (as suggested by Bruce Moseley et al.[89]), do we need surgeons to have training beyond merely not hurting patients?

Placebo treatments fall into a regulatory gray zone. Consider the use of OLP for IBS. The tangible component of the treatment amounts to a bottle of placebo pills. Should OLPs fall under the jurisdiction of the FDA in the United States on a par with other pharmaceuticals? Should the FDA have a role in regulating patients' beliefs and expectations, clinicians' demeanor, and other contextual cues? Given the fact that the working of OLPs has little to do with pharmacokinetics, an organization that is designed to oversee chemical interactions seems to be an awkward supervision choice.

5.4 Placebos and the Meaning of Life

The effects of placebos have often been dismissed as merely subjective. The dramatic effects of placebo therapies force us to question the clinical goals of medicine. Should we care mostly about restoring proper bodily functions or improving patients' subjective experiences? Of course, the two are often connected with the former causing the latter. Still, there are instances where one can feel better without necessarily experiencing any changes at the pathological level. This tension is certainly not new in medicine. The debate between psychoanalysis (discovering and addressing the root cause of one's neuroses) and behaviorism (focusing primarily on mitigating surface symptoms) involves a similar dynamic. The fact remains that all of us live for a finite amount of time. If we can ensure that our time on Earth is filled with positive subjective experiences, what difference does it make if our anatomy is falling apart? To be fair, focusing solely on current subjective experiences might very well ignore troubles down the road. By not addressing underlying pathologies, one might live a shorter life or trade a comfortable present for a miserable future. But maximizing one's lifespan is certainly not universally desired. Many of us would rather live a shorter life if it is of a higher quality. The duality of placebo therapies forces us to question the orthodox emphasis that we *are* sick as long as the physiological sickness remains – the fact that you do not feel sick is not a mark of being healthy.

Clinical medicine is but one of many tools to restore and to maximize our well-being. To live a perfectly healthy life devoid of ailments is clearly attractive to many of us. But perfect health is hardly worth maintaining for its own sake; it is but a canvas for a good life. Without the opportunities and the capacity to live well, a functioning body is like a pair of pristine hiking boots. To craft a meaningful and well-lived life, it is necessary, at the very least, to know how a life can be lived in all its diversity and intricacy. The joy of playing a musical instrument can only be experienced if the person has access to an instrument and the time to play it. Having never played an instrument, they might not know that they wished to live the life of a musician. To make an authentic decision about how one should live, it is imperative to be exposed to how life can be lived. In other words, one needs the time and the resources to learn ways to live.

In his essay "In Praise of Idleness," Bertrand Russell argues that the increased productivity gained from automation ought to be converted to expand the public's ability to live a more leisurely life.[90] Education plays an important role in providing us with the tools necessary to enjoy life intelligently, Russell goes on to point out. Learning how to read, for instance, creates the possibility of deriving joy and meaning from literary works. A central role of education, according to him, is to provide us with the skills necessary to experience the world in ways that we would not have noticed otherwise.

If medicine is in the business of helping us to live our lives well, it must recognize that biological health (e.g., organs functioning normally) is not intrinsically valuable. Health is but one of many components that are essential to a life lived well. As long as we can sustain well-being, it matters little whether underlying physiological functions are at their biological norms. In this regard, the fact that some placebo therapies confer improved subjective experiences while doing little to change the underlying physiology is very much in line with the main tenets of holistic medicine; that is, treating patients as whole individuals as opposed to mere bundles of conditions. As research into placebo therapies continues, perhaps we can keep in mind that a life well-lived requires a life lived.

5.5 Why Placebos Should Fascinate Philosophers

My research into placebos began after attending a presentation by Ted Kaptchuk. His experimental results conflicted with what I thought I knew about placebo effects and medicine in general. As I continued reading more about placebo research, the challenges that many researchers have encountered struck me as clearly philosophical in nature. Untangling the conceptual mess comes naturally for any competent philosopher. Not only are these tasks interesting in and of themselves, they also concern a fascinating area of medicine. And, like clinical ethics, progress made at the philosophical level can have tangible benefits. From sharpening the methodology of a placebo-controlled clinical trial to examining the alleged differences between placebo causal paths and nonplacebo ones, good philosophy can help create better medicine.

In the course of learning more about placebo effects, it also became apparent that research and clinical medicine rarely travel along clean methodological paths. Post-Kuhnians are right. Science is practiced by real people guided by personal agendas, social pressures, and the demands of the real world. To ignore these features and focus entirely on a sanitized version of science can only further remove the contribution philosophers can make. The often frustrating reality of medical practice that violates its own commitment to being evidence-based and enacts divisions nudged by financial interests and historic inertia can be jarring to philosophers who are fond of the "desert landscape." Placebo research vividly highlights many of these less admirable elements of clinical and medical research. For anyone who believes in the importance of research-as-activism and who strives to make the world a better place, placebo research is an entry point where philosophical skills in ethics, philosophy of science, epistemology, and metaphysics can be put to their maximal usage.

This Element has surveyed three usages of placebo: as a way to placate patients, as clinical controls, and as therapies. We also looked at some noteworthy studies that lay the groundwork for an empirically informed examination of placebos and placebo effects. I argued that in comparison to classical conditioning and expectancy, the BBM$^+$ presents a more plausible account of placebic mechanisms. Placebo effects necessitate a reexamination of what constitutes a treatment. Moreover, given the conceptual messiness of background theories in medicine whose acceptance is often driven by pragmatic reasons, defining *placebo* and *placebo effects* on the basis of these theories would leave us with the same characteristics. Previous attempts to define placebo-related terms have failed because they looked for definitions that are devoid of pragmatic influences. Placebos and placebo effects represent conceptual points where the system of conventional medicine "breaks." Rather than stigmatizing placebo phenomena, these failure points can teach us a great deal about the goals of healthcare, the nature of treatments, and ultimately who we are. It is here that the humanists can be of great help.

Notes

1. Reeves et al. 2007.
2. Jensen et al. 2012.
3. Mill 1882, 280.
4. Aronson 1999.
5. Hooper 1817, 634.
6. Houston 1938.
7. Sherman & Hickner 2008.
8. Beecher 1955.
9. Beecher 1955, 1605.
10. Some scholars call the net outcome of the placebo-controlled arm "placebo response." This is an unfortunate word choice that risks increasing the confusion between placebo effects and the net outcome of the placebo-controlled arm. Instead of "placebo response," "control arm response" might be a better term.
11. Wendler & Miller 2004.
12. Sandler, Glesne, & Bodfish 2010.
13. Kaptchuk et al. 2010.
14. Kaptchuk et al. 2010, e15591.
15. Beecher 1946.
16. Beecher 1955, 1606.
17. Hróbjartsson & Gøtzsche 2001.
18. Kienle & Kiene 1997, 1312.
19. See Kappauf et al. 1997 for a case study of SR.
20. de la Vega et al. 2017.
21. Amanzio & Benedetti 1999.
22. Levine, Gordon, & Fields 1978.
23. Kirchhof et al. 2018.
24. Diamond et al. 2006.
25. Kallmes et al. 2009.
26. Bootle 2014.
27. See Hróbjartsson & Gøtzsche 2001 and Hróbjartsson & Gøtzsche 2004.
28. Hróbjartsson & Gøtzsche 2004, 91.
29. Hróbjartsson & Gøtzsche 2010, 14–15.
30. Foster et al. 2004.
31. Kam-Hansen et al. 2014.
32. de Craen et al. 1996.
33. Cattaneo, Lucchelli, & Filippucci 1970.
34. Lucchelli, Cattaneo, & Zattoni 1978.
35. Moerman 2017.
36. Waber et al. 2008.
37. Branthwaite & Cooper 1981.
38. Buckalew & Coffield 1982.

39. Steinkopf 2015.
40. Benedetti 2013 provides an evolutionary account of placebo effects. He traces the emergence of the institution of healing to the altruistic practice of allogrooming (social grooming within a group).
41. While Pavlov has been credited with the discovery of classical conditioning, there is ample evidence that other scholars including the late psychologist Edwin Twitmyer might have done so before Pavlov. In his 1902 dissertation, Edwin Twitmyer paired the ringing of a bell with jerk-inducing strikes of subjects' knees. After sufficient exposure, he conditioned his subjects so that their knees would jerk when he rang the bell. His results were presented in 1904 in front of William James at the American Psychological Association, the same year Pavlov presented his salivating dog experiment. See Rosenzweig 1960 and Coon 1982.
42. Herrnstein 1962, 678.
43. Linde et al. 2005; Witt et al. 2005; Brinkhaus et al. 2006.
44. Kaptchuk et al. 2009.
45. Lidstone et al. 2010.
46. Kaptchuk et al. 2009.
47. Hawkins & Blakeslee 2007, 159.
48. Jung et al. 2017.
49. Arandia & Di Paolo 2022.
50. Kirsch 2018.
51. Vase et al. 2003.
52. See Clark 2013 for a brilliant and detailed overview of the Bayesian brain.
53. Yon, Heyes, & Press 2020.
54. Jensen et al. 2012.
55. See Prioleau, Murdock, & Brody 1983 and Gaab, Locher, & Blease 2018.
56. Moerman 2000 has a fascinating discussion of examples of cultural variations in placebo effects.
57. Both my use of "narrative" and that of narrative medicine share a key idea: a patient's narrative can help them make sense of their ailment and suffering.
58. A study by Locher et al. 2017 concluded that subjects who were told the rationale of an OLP treatment performed better than those who were not told the rationale.
59. Chavarria et al. 2017.
60. Thomson 1982.
61. Shapiro 1964, 57.
62. Häuser, Hansen, & Enck 2012, 460.
63. Some natural remedies that I knew of as a child in Hong Kong were superbly effective for infections. It was not until chemical analyses were done years later that it was discovered that they contained large doses of conventional antibiotics.
64. See Ho 2012 for a discussion of the controversies surrounding the use of antidepressants in adolescents.

65. Lasagna 1955 defines placebo as "an inactive, harmless pill or injection which is given solely for its psychological effect on the patient" (68).
66. Brody 2018, 353.
67. Engel 1977, 132.
68. Howick 2017.
69. Grünbaum 1986.
70. Greenwood 1997.
71. Howick 2017, 1379.
72. Fontanarosa & Lundberg 1998.
73. American Psychiatric Association 2013.
74. Mulinari 2018.
75. Hirschauer 1998.
76. I thank Mason Kortz for this suggestion.
77. Yu 2018.
78. Before we fine-tune experimental methodologies to capture some of the nuances of placebo effects, it is important to note that posttrial confirmation of blinding is rarely done. In Hróbjartsson et al.'s 2007 study, they concluded that only 2 percent of clinical trials checked that blinding was successful. When researchers evaluate blinding success in, say, posttrial surveys, the methods are seldom robust enough to provide meaningful evidence. See Bang, Ni, & Davis 2004.
79. Boehm et al. 2017; Weijer 2002.
80. Lasagna et al. 1954.
81. Lasagna et al. 1954, 775.
82. Geers et al. 2005.
83. See Worrall 2007 for an in-depth critique of the standard hierarchy of evidence in medicine.
84. Smieliauskas, Lam, & Howard 2014.
85. Howick et al. 2013.
86. Li et al., 777.
87. I learned of this example from Worrall 2016.
88. Connett 2015.
89. Moseley et al. 2002.
90. Russell 1932.

References

Amanzio, M, Benedetti, F. Neuropharmacological Dissection of Placebo Analgesia: Expectation-Activated Opioid Systems versus Conditioning-Activated Specific Subsystems. *Journal of Neuroscience* 19 (1999): 484–94.

American Psychiatric Association. *Diagnostic and Statistical Manual of Mental Disorders (DSM-5®)*. Washington, DC: American Psychiatric Publishing, 2013.

Arandia, IR, Di Paolo, EA. On Symptom Perception, Placebo Effects, and the Bayesian Brain. *PAIN* 163 (2022): e604. https://doi.org/10.1097/j.pain.00000 00000002488.

Aronson, J. Please, Please Me. *BMJ (Clinical Research Edition)* 318 (1999): 716.

Bang, H, Ni, L, Davis, CE. Assessment of Blinding in Clinical Trials. *Controlled Clinical Trials* 25 (2004): 143–56.

Beecher, HK. Pain in Men Wounded in Battle. *Annals of Surgery* 123 (1946): 96–105.

Beecher, HK. The Powerful Placebo. *JAMA* 159 (1955): 1602–6.

Benedetti, F. Placebo and the New Physiology of the Doctor–Patient Relationship. *Physiological Reviews* 93 (2013): 1207–46.

Boehm, K, Berger, B, Weger, U, Heusser, P. Does the Model of Additive Effect in Placebo Research Still Hold True? A Narrative Review. *JRSM Open* 8 (2017): 2054270416681434. 10.1177/2054270416681434.

Bootle, O. The Power of the Placebo. *BBC Horizon* (2014). www.bbc.co.uk/programmes/p01s6fcx.

Branthwaite, A, Cooper, P. Analgesic Effects of Branding in Treatment of Headaches. *BMJ (Clinical Research Edition)* 282 (1981): 1576–8.

Brinkhaus, B, Witt, CM, Jena, S, et al. Acupuncture in Patients with Chronic Low Back Pain: A Randomized Controlled Trial. *Archive of Internal Medicine* 166 (2006): 450–7.

Brody, H. Meaning and an Overview of the Placebo Effect. *Perspectives in Biology and Medicine* 61 (2018): 353–60.

Buckalew, LW, Coffield, KE. An Investigation of Drug Expectancy as a Function of Capsule Color and Size and Preparation Form. *Journal of Clinical Psychopharmacology* 2 (1982): 245–8.

Cattaneo, AD, Lucchelli, PE, Filippucci, G. Sedative Effects of Placebo Treatment. *European Journal of Clinical Pharmacology* 3 (1970): 43–5.

Chavarria, V, Vian, J, Pereira, C, et al. The Placebo and Nocebo Phenomena: Their Clinical Management and Impact on Treatment Outcomes. *Clinical Therapeutics* 39 (2017): 477–86.

Clark, A. Whatever Next? Predictive Brains, Situated Agents, and the Future of Cognitive Science. *Behavioral and Brain Sciences* 36 (2013): 181–204.

Connett, D. Exposed: The Painkiller Labelling Scam. *The Independent*, December 15, 2015. www.pressreader.com/uk/the-independent-1029/20151215/281479275361745/TextView.

Coon, DJ. Eponymy, Obscurity, Twitmyer, and Pavlov. *Journal of the History of the Behavioral Sciences* 18 (1982): 255–62.

de Craen, AJM, Roos, PJ, De Vries, AL, Kleijnen, J. Effect of Colour of Drugs: Systematic Review of Perceived Effect of Drugs and of Their Effectiveness. *BMJ* 313 (1996): 1624–6.

de la Vega, R, Alberti, S, Ruíz-Barquín, R, Soós, I, Szabo, A. Induced Beliefs about a Fictive Energy Drink Influences 200-M Sprint Performance. *European Journal of Sport Science* 17 (2017): 1084–9. https://doi.org/10.1080/17461391.2017.1339735.

Diamond, TH, Bryant, C, Browne, L, Clark, WA. Clinical Outcomes after Acute Osteoporotic Vertebral Fractures: A 2-Year Non-Randomised Trial Comparing Percutaneous Vertebroplasty with Conservative Therapy. *Medical Journal of Australia* 184 (2006): 113–17.

Engel, GL. The Need for a New Medical Model: A Challenge for Biomedicine. *Science* 196 (1977): 129–36.

Fontanarosa, PB, Lundberg, G. Alternative Medicine Meets Science. *JAMA* 280 (1998): 1618–19.

Foster, KA, Liskin, J, Cen, S, et al. The Trager Approach in the Treatment of Chronic Headache: A Pilot Study. *Alternative Therapies in Health and Medicine* 10 (2004): 40–6.

Gaab, J, Locher, C, Blease, C. Placebo and Psychotherapy: Differences, Similarities, and Implications. *International Review of Neurobiology* 138 (2018): 241–55.

Geers, AL, Helfer, SG, Kosbab, K, Weiland, PE, Landry, SJ. Reconsidering the Role of Personality in Placebo Effects: Dispositional Optimism, Situational Expectations, and the Placebo Response. *Journal of Psychosomatic Research* 58 (2005): 121–7.

Greenwood, JD. Placebo Control Treatments and the Evaluation of Psychotherapy: A Reply to Grünbaum and Erwin. *Philosophy of Science* 64 (1997): 497–510.

Grünbaum, A. The Placebo Concept in Medicine and Psychiatry. *Psychological Medicine* 16 (1986): 19–38.

Häuser, W, Hansen, E, Enck, P. Nocebo Phenomena in Medicine: Their Relevance in Everyday Clinical Practice. *Deutsches Ärzteblatt International* 109 (2012): 459–65.

Hawkins, J, Blakeslee, S. *On Intelligence: How a New Understanding of the Brain Will Lead to the Creation of Truly Intelligent Machines.* New York: Henry Holt and Company, 2007.

Herrnstein, RJ. Placebo Effect in the Rat. *Science* 138 (1962): 677–8.

Hirschauer, S. Performing Sexes and Genders in Medical Practices. In Berg, M, Mol, A, editors. *Differences in Medicine: Unraveling Practices, Techniques, and Bodies.* Durham, NC: Duke University Press, 1998. pp. 13–27.

Ho, D. Antidepressants and the FDA's Black-Box Warning: Determining a Rational Public Policy in the Absence of Sufficient Evidence. *Virtual Mentor – The American Medical Association Journal of Ethics* 14 (2012): 483–8.

Hooper, R. *Quincy's Lexicon-Medicum : A New Medical Dictionary, Containing an Explanation of the Terms in Anatomy, Physiology, Practice of Physic, Materia Medica, Chymistry, Pharmacy, Surgery, Midwifery, and the Various Branches of Natural Philosophy Connected with Medicine. Selected, Arranged, and Compiled, from the Best Authors by Robert Hooper.* Philadelphia, PA: Benjamin Warner, M. Carey & Son, and Edward Parker, 1817.

Houston, WR. The Doctor Himself as a Therapeutic Agent. *Annals of Internal Medicine* 11 (1938): 1416–25.

Howick, J. The Relativity of "Placebos": Defending a Modified Version of Grünbaum's Definition. *Synthese* 194 (2017): 1363–96.

Howick, J, Friedemann, C, Tsakok, M, et al. Are Treatments More Effective Than Placebos? A Systematic Review and Meta-Analysis. *PLoS One* 8 (2013): e62599. https://doi.org/10.1371/journal.pone.0062599.

Hróbjartsson, A, Gøtzsche, PC. Is the Placebo Powerless? *New England Journal of Medicine* 344 (2001): 1594–602.

Hróbjartsson, A, Gøtzsche, PC. Is the Placebo Powerless? Update of a Systematic Review with 52 New Randomized Trials Comparing Placebo with No Treatment. *Journal of Internal Medicine* 256 (2004): 91–100.

Hróbjartsson, A, Gøtzsche, PC. Placebo Interventions for All Clinical Conditions. *Cochrane Database of Systematic Reviews* 1 (2010): Cd003974. https://doi.org/10.1002/14651858.CD003974.pub3.

Hróbjartsson, A, Forfang, E, Haahr, MT, Als-Nielsen, B, Brorson, S. Blinded Trials Taken to the Test: An Analysis of Randomized Clinical Trials That Report Tests for the Success of Blinding. *International Journal of Epidemiology* 36 (2007): 654–63.

Jensen, KB, Kaptchuk, TJ, Kirsch, I, Raicek, J, Lindstrom, KM, Berna, C, Gollub, RL, Ingvar, M, Kong, J. Nonconscious Activation of Placebo and Nocebo Pain Responses. *Proceedings of the National Academy of Sciences of the United States of America* 109 (2012): 15959–64.

Jung, W-M, Lee, Y-S, Wallraven, C, Chae, Y. Bayesian Prediction of Placebo Analgesia in an Instrumental Learning Model. *PLoS ONE* 12 (2017): e0172609. https://doi.org/10.1371/journal.pone.0172609.

Kallmes, DF, Comstock, BA, Heagerty, PJ, et al. A Randomized Trial of Vertebroplasty for Osteoporotic Spinal Fractures. *New England Journal of Medicine* 361 (2009): 569–79.

Kam-Hansen, S, Jakubowski, M, Kelley, JM et al. Altered Placebo and Drug Labeling Changes the Outcome of Episodic Migraine Attacks. *Science Translational Medicine* 6 (2014): 218ra5. https://doi.org/10.1126/sci translmed.3006175.

Kappauf, H, Gallmeier, WM, Wünsch, PH, et al. Complete Spontaneous Remission in a Patient with Metastatic Non-Small-Cell Lung Cancer: Case Report, Review of Literature, and Discussion of Possible Biological Pathways Involved. *Annals of Oncology* 8 (1997): 1031–9.

Kaptchuk, TJ, Friedlander, E, Kelley, JM, et al. Placebos without Deception: A Randomized Controlled Trial in Irritable Bowel Syndrome. *PLoS One* 5 (2010): e15591. https://doi.org/10.1371/journal.pone.0015591.

Kaptchuk, TJ, Shaw, J, Kerr, CE, et al. "Maybe I Made up the Whole Thing": Placebos and Patients' Experiences in a Randomized Controlled Trial. *Culture, Medicine and Psychiatry* 33 (2009): 382–411.

Kienle, GS, Kiene, H. The Powerful Placebo Effect: Fact or Fiction? *Journal of Clinical Epidemiology* 50 (1997): 1311–18.

Kirchhof, J, Petrakova, L, Brinkhoff, A, et al. Learned Immunosuppressive Placebo Responses in Renal Transplant Patients. *Proceedings of the National Academy of Sciences of the United States of America* 115 (2018): 4223–7.

Kirsch, I. Response Expectancy and the Placebo Effect. *International Review of Neurobiology* 138 (2018): 81–93.

Lasagna, L. Placebos. *Scientific American* 193 (1955): 68–71.

Lasagna, L, Mosteller, F, von Felsinger, JM, Beecher, HK. A Study of the Placebo Response. *American Journal of Medicine* 16 (1954): 770–9.

Levine, J, Gordon, N, Fields, H. The Mechanism of Placebo Analgesia. *Lancet* 312 (1978): 654–7.

Li, S, Stampfer, MJ, Williams, DR, Vanderweele, TJ. Association of Religious Service Attendance with Mortality among Women. *JAMA Internal Medicine* 176 (2016): 777-85.

Lidstone, SC, Schulzer, M, Dinelle, K, et al. Effects of Expectation on Placebo-Induced Dopamine Release in Parkinson Disease. *Archives of General Psychiatry* 67 (2010): 857–65.

Linde, K, Streng, A, Jurgens, S, et al. Acupuncture for Patients with Migraine: A Randomized Controlled Trial. *JAMA* 293 (2005): 2118–25.

Locher, C, Frey Nascimento, A, Kirsch, I, et al. Is the Rationale More Important Than Deception? A Randomized Controlled Trial of Open-Label Placebo Analgesia. *Pain* 158 (2017): 2320–8.

Lucchelli, PE, Cattaneo, AD, Zattoni, J. Effect of Capsule Colour and Order of Administration of Hypnotic Treatments. *European Journal of Clinical Pharmacology* 13 (1978): 153–5.

Mill, JS. *A System of Logic, Ratiocinative and Inductive, Being a Connected View of the Principle of Evidence, and the Methods of Scientific Investigation.* 8th ed. New York: Harper & Brothers, 1882.

Moerman, DE. Cultural Variations in the Placebo Effect: Ulcers, Anxiety, and Blood Pressure. *Medical Anthropology Quarterly* 14 (2000): 51–72.

Moerman, DE. Philosophy and "Placebo" Analgesia. In Corns, J, editor. *The Routledge Handbook of Philosophy of Pain.* New York: Routledge, 2017, pp. 378–87.

Moseley, JB, O'Malley, K, Petersen, NJ, et al. A Controlled Trial of Arthroscopic Surgery for Osteoarthritis of the Knee. *New England Journal of Medicine* 347 (2002): 81–8.

Mulinari, S. Let the Drugs Lead the Way! On the Unfolding of a Research Program in Psychiatry. *Philosophy, Psychiatry, & Psychology* 25 (2018): 289–302.

Prioleau, L, Murdock, M, Brody, N. An Analysis of Psychotherapy versus Placebo Studies. *Behavioral and Brain Sciences* 6 (1983): 275–85.

Reeves, RR, Ladner, ME, Hart, RH, Burke, RS. Nocebo Effects with Antidepressant Clinical Drug Trial Placebos. *General Hospital Psychiatry* 29 (2007): 275–7.

Rosenzweig, MR. Pavlov, Bechterev, and Twitmyer on Conditioning. *American Journal of Psychology* 73 (1960): 312–16.

Russell, B. In Praise of Idleness. *Harper's Magazine*, October, 1932.

Sandler, AD, Glesne, CE, Bodfish, JW. Conditioned Placebo Dose Reduction: A New Treatment in Attention-Deficit Hyperactivity Disorder? *Journal of Developmental and Behavioral Pediatrics* 31 (2010): 369–75.

Shapiro, AK. A Historic and Heuristic Definition of the Placebo. *Psychiatry* 27 (1964): 52–8.

Sherman, R, Hickner, J. Academic Physicians Use Placebos in Clinical Practice and Believe in the Mind–Body Connection. *Journal of General Internal Medicine* 23 (2008): 7–10.

Smieliauskas, F, Lam, S, Howard, DH. Impact of Negative Clinical Trial Results for Vertebroplasty on Vertebral Augmentation Procedure Rates. *Journal of the American College of Surgeons* 219 (2014): 525–33.e1. http://dx.doi.org/10.1016/j.jamcollsurg.2014.03.047.

Steinkopf, L. The Signaling Theory of Symptoms: An Evolutionary Explanation of the Placebo Effect. *Evolutionary Psychology* 13 (2015): 1474704915600559. https://doi.org/10.1177/1474704915600559.

Thomson, R. Side Effects and Placebo Amplification. *British Journal of Psychiatry* 140 (1982): 64–8.

Vase, L, Robinson, ME, Verne, GN, Price, DD. The Contributions of Suggestion, Desire, and Expectation to Placebo Effects in Irritable Bowel Syndrome Patients. An Empirical Investigation. *Pain* 105 (2003): 17–25.

Waber, RL, Shiv, B, Carmon, Z, Ariely, D. Commercial Features of Placebo and Therapeutic Efficacy. *JAMA* 299 (2008): 1016–17.

Weijer, C. I Need a Placebo Like I Need a Hole in the Head. *Journal of Law, Medicine & Ethics: A Journal of the American Society of Law, Medicine & Ethics* 30 (2002): 69–72.

Wendler, D, Miller, FG. Deception in the Pursuit of Science. *Archives of Internal Medicine* 164 (2004): 597–600.

Witt, C, Brinkhaus, B, Jena, S, et al. Acupuncture in Patients with Osteoarthritis of the Knee: A Randomised Trial. *Lancet* 366 (2005): 136–43.

Worrall, J. Evidence in Medicine and Evidence-Based Medicine. *Philosophy Compass* 2 (2007): 981–1022.

Worrall, J. The Placebo Effect and Evidence-Based Policy. Department of Philosophy, Logic and Scientific Method, London School of Economics, January 13, 2016. www.lse.ac.uk/philosophy/blog/2016/01/13/the-placebo-effect-and-evidence-based-policy/.

Yon, D, Heyes, C, Press, C. Beliefs and Desires in the Predictive Brain. *Nature Communications* 11 (2020): 4404. https://doi.org/10.1038/s41467-020-18332-9.

Yu, C. The Future of Work: Placebo. *Wired*, December 17, 2018. www.wired.com/story/future-of-work-placebo-charles-yu/.

Acknowledgments

My research would not have been possible without the support of Dean Delia Anderson and Provost Caroline Zeind of my home institution, Massachusetts College of Pharmacy and Health Sciences. This Element was largely written during my sabbatical leave in the fall of 2022. I thank Professor Anna Elsner for organizing my stay at the Institute of Biomedical Ethics and History of Science at the University of Zurich. A visit to the University of Akureyri in Iceland also afforded me an opportunity to share my research with experts there. I extend my gratitude to Professor Sigurður Kristinsson for making the arrangements. Bradley Monton's comments on earlier drafts benefited the project greatly. Professor Anya Plutynski provided invaluable comments as well. I remain in awe of her brilliance and generosity. My father-in-law Peter Leo served once again as my editor. I dedicate this Element to him and to Sylvia, my mother-in-law.

Cambridge Elements ≡

Bioethics and Neuroethics

Thomasine Kushner

California Pacific Medical Center, San Francisco

Thomasine Kushner, PhD, is the founding Editor of the *Cambridge Quarterly of Healthcare Ethics* and coordinates the International Bioethics Retreat, where bioethicists share their current research projects, the Cambridge Consortium for Bioethics Education, a growing network of global bioethics educators, and the Cambridge–ICM Neuroethics Network, which provides a setting for leading brain scientists and ethicists to learn from each other.

About the Series

Bioethics and neuroethics play pivotal roles in today's debates in philosophy, science, law, and health policy. With the rapid growth of scientific and technological advances, their importance will only increase. This series provides focused and comprehensive coverage in both disciplines consisting of foundational topics, current subjects under discussion and views toward future developments.

Cambridge Elements ☰

Bioethics and Neuroethics

Elements in the Series

Roles of Justice in Bioethics
Matti Hayry

The Ethics of Consciousness
Walter Glannon

Responsibility for Health
Sven Ove Hansson

Controlling Love: The Ethics and Desirability of Using 'Love Drugs'
Peter Herissone-Kelly

Immune Ethics
Walter Glannon

What Placebos Teach Us about Health and Care: A Philosopher Pops a Pill
Dien Ho

A full series listing is available at: www.cambridge.org/EBAN

Printed in the United States
by Baker & Taylor Publisher Services